T4-ADP-793

ALSO BY GEORGE M. BROCKWAY, PhD

Some Thoughts on the Big Questions   (Bk. 1)

A Spiritual Guide for Retirement   (Bk. 2)

A *Letter* to My Grandchildren   (Bk. 3)

Essays in Search of Understanding   (Bk. 4)

Musings Before We Die

George M. Brockway, Ph.D.

authorHOUSE

AuthorHouse™
1663 Liberty Drive
Bloomington, IN 47403
www.authorhouse.com
Phone: 833-262-8899

© *2024 George M. Brockway, Ph.D. All rights reserved.*

No part of this book may be reproduced, stored in a retrieval system, or transmitted by any means without the written permission of the author.

Published by AuthorHouse 01/19/2024

ISBN: 979-8-8230-1941-5 (sc)
ISBN: 979-8-8230-1942-2 (e)

Library of Congress Control Number: 2023923957

Print information available on the last page.

Any people depicted in stock imagery provided by Getty Images are models, and such images are being used for illustrative purposes only.
Certain stock imagery © Getty Images.

This book is printed on acid-free paper.

Because of the dynamic nature of the Internet, any web addresses or links contained in this book may have changed since publication and may no longer be valid. The views expressed in this work are solely those of the author and do not necessarily reflect the views of the publisher, and the publisher hereby disclaims any responsibility for them.

"So Socrates!" he teased, "you are still saying the same things I heard you say long ago." Socrates replied: "It is more terrifying than that: not only am I always saying the same things, but also *about* the same things."

(Xenophon, *Memorabilia* IV.4.6)

And, alas, so also am I.

Much thanks to Jonathan Lear who put me on to this epigram in his book: *Imagining the End – Mourning and Ethical Life*. I adopt it here because it so aptly captures what I'm doing in this book and which is indicated by the multiple references to my other books in the Table of Contents.

Musings Before We Die

Ch.	Contents	Pg.
1.	<u>The One Question that opens . . or closes the most important 'doors' (subjects)</u>.	1
2.	<u>Does Anything Spiritual Exist?</u> See also: Bk 1, Ch. 4 & Bk. 4, Ch. 3	11
3.	<u>What are you willing to accept *as evidence for* or *against* the spiritual?</u>	19
	History	
	Argument See also: Bk. 3, Ch. 2;	
	Experience See also: Bk. 2, Ch. 5;	
4.	<u>But any (and every) experience involves *interpretation* which results in . . .</u>	41
5.	<u>Moderate Realism (a dualism) vs. Idealism (a monism).</u> See also: Bk. 2, Ch. 11	
	& Bk. 4, Ch. 7;	49
6.	<u>An Important Distinction and Its Impact.</u>	63
7.	<u>Don't be so open-minded that your brains fall out.</u>	71
	Part 1 – No-self; Part 2 – The Two Truths Doctrine;	
	Part 3 – Shutting down the discursive, analytic mind.	
8.	<u>*Why* did the universe begin?</u> (Cp. *Why* is there something rather than nothing?)	85
9.	<u>Dear Dalai Lama, "Agreed, but then, and by the same token, how *can* something physical come from something spiritual, something material from something *im*material?"</u>	97
10.	<u>*Why* be kind?</u> See also: Bk. 1, Ch's 8, 10 & Bk. 4, Ch. 9	107
11.	<u>Must there be a lasting and good end-state for our lives to have meaning and value</u>?	115
12.	With respect to making the world a better place to live, does the religious worldview add anything important to the secular humanist worldview?	
	See also: Bk. 2, Ch's 4, 5&7;	123

INTRODUCTION

This book considers some questions which people have struggled with over the centuries in their effort to figure out what their human life is all about, what meaning it has, if any, and what, if anything, happens next. One of the reasons they have engaged in this struggle is the desire to understand, to put into context and to find meaning in their existence. And it seems to me that pursuing those goals is both worthwhile and, perhaps even more important, something that will enrich the life of anyone who makes the effort. And thus, one of the things you should try to do before you die.

This is not a "How To" book. Rather, it's a "here's something to think about" book. The questions we'll be looking at deal with issues concerning your "you" or your *self* and whether that you is anything substantial or anything at all, and what might happen to that "you" after the death of your body. They deal with the way reality is structured, more precisely, with the way non-physical reality is structured, if there is any such. And whether there is any such. They deal with the spiritual and consciousness and mind, but these latter two not from the viewpoint of the physical sciences. Rather, these questions are seeking to understand what is true and what we should believe about our **selves** and the kind of existence these selves have and might have in the future.

And so, the fuller title for this book might have been: **The Questions You May Want to Explore Before You Die**. But that seemed too clumsy and long, so I've shortened it to the title above. I am assuming that most of us are curious about such things as: whether our lives are meaningful and important? And if so, what makes them such?

And if not, how should (does?) that affect the way we live or should live? Is this life all there is for each of us or will we, in some way(s), continue to exist after the death of our body? And how does/should an answer either way affect the choices we make, what we think is really important, how we treat other people, how we understand our actions in the here-and-now and whether there is any connection between how we live in the here and now and whatever might happen to us next.

At this point we could divide the world into two different groups of people. Those who have not yet considered such questions to their own satisfaction but do wish to do so, and those who have thought about those sorts of things and have come to conclusions about them that satisfy themselves. To the first group, I say 'welcome, I hope you will find these thoughts and reflections to be helpful in your quest. And to the second group, I would suggest that this advice columnist has some wisdom to offer all of us.

> "If you're unwilling to question whether you're wrong, then there's little chance you'll be right."
> Caroline Hax, *WP* 10/11/09

****

A word about how the book is structured.

Each chapter is prefaced with a one page outline of what the chapter is about, the major parts that chapter is broken into and, most importantly, the connections between and within those parts. This is meant to be helpful to the reader both in deciding whether they want to continue reading that chapter (at that time) and in following the flow of thought when they do read the chapter.

Chapter Outline   **Chapter 1**

Is there anything you can do now that will affect what happens to you after you die?

Some of the topics this question (or the answers to it) opens . . . or closes:

1. "You" – or one's 'self'? Does such (a 'self') even exist? And if so, to what does it refer?

    The most common options: . . . .

    > Something substantial and lasting or merely a temporary conglomeration of constantly changing attributes *designated as* one's 'self' for convenience sake?

2. Consciousness and the 'self'. Can there be a 'self' without consciousness? And what is consciousness? Does <u>anything</u> which is conscious have a 'self'? **Self-consciousness.**

3. <u>Is there</u> any *personal* existence, does any 'self' survive *after* the death of the body? Could one ever *know* such a thing? In this life?

    > Does **any such realm or reality** (one that is non-corporeal, i.e. a **"spiritual" realm or reality**) actually exist? And again, can one ever *know* such a thing? (See Ch. 2)

4. If one's self does persist beyond the death of the body, does/should that affect how one lives? Depends on whether what we do now affects what happens after the death of the body.

    > (And **implies** we have some choice about and power over how we live, = **free will**.)

    Does one have to act/live in a particular way, or achieve a particular insight, in order to get **"there"**?

    > "There" as a state of being or as knowing the transcendent?
    > "There" before death and "there" after death.
    > And does this imply different ways of being in such an 'after life'.

5. A bit more on Free Will.

Chapter 1
Is there anything you can do now that will affect what happens to you after you die?

Here are just some of the /subjects involved in trying to answer this question. What does the "you" refer to? (I'll assume throughout that it refers to the same thing as one's **self**.) But is there such a 'thing' as our self? If there is, of what is it composed? Or, in order to not beg any questions, how is it most accurately described? What is its nature? What sort of a 'thing' is it? Is it anything substantial?

And how is it related to one's consciousness? Indeed, **what is consciousness**? And, to be clear, I am not assuming that anything will, in fact, happen to this 'you' after you die. It's a question. So it is, in effect, also asking whether or not there is anything, any sort of personal existence, after one's death. And, of course, if anything does happen to our *self* after the death of our body, then that would seem to require some sort of **spiritual realm** or **spiritual reality**. How is that to be understood? What would that be like? And what evidence is there, if any, that any such realm or reality actually exists? And finally, the question implies that there might be **some connection between how we live in the here-and-now and what happens to us after we die**. Woah! Those are a lot of pretty significant questions. Questions and topics which people have struggled over for millennia! And since the question that heads this chapter involves all of these subsequent topics and questions, it might very well be thought of as, if not "the", at least "a" very important question.

****

1. So let's start by examining the whole notion of **the *self*.** One's you. To what does this refer? Well, I would start with: it refers to one's character plus one's personality; to one's abilities, desires, inclinations, history, and to one's patterns and habits of thought and behavior (= character?). This would normally include what is usually referred to as one's will and one's mind. A couple of our more obvious and important faculties or abilities.

I would also say that this 'entity'/subject is constantly changing. As our history proceeds and our abilities grow and change, our knowledge base and experience expand, our character and personality change accordingly. So one's *self* is not a fixed, never changing, entity. And yet, **there is a recognizable continuity** to one's *self*. Recognizable to us and by our friends, neighbors and loved ones.

So, is this *self* something substantial and lasting or merely a temporary conglomeration of constantly changing attributes *designated as* "a self" for convenience sake? Well, that depends, of course, on what one means by "substantial". If one means by the term that it (one's *self*) is something that does not and cannot change, then "no", it (as just described) is not substantial since it is constantly changing. Not wholly so, but in part. But if one means by "substantial" that it is a necessary component of one's unique personhood, then "yes", it is substantial. And if one means by "substantial" that you can't lose it all together and still remain a person, then "yes" it is substantial.

Another possible meaning for "substantial" might be: that it exists of its own accord; it needs nothing else in order to exist. Classically, however, only one thing meets that definition of "substantial", viz. God or That-Which-Exists-Necessarily. And no one, that I know of, has ever claimed that for one's *self*. So, the *self* is not substantial in that sense either.

Is the *self* something physical? Well, if it were, we could, at least theoretically, put our finger on it or a pin in it. But we can't do that, so "no" it is not anything physical. I would say it exists more like an ability exists. E.g., someone might have what we call an innate ability to learn languages or to excel at mathematics. Indeed, energy itself has been defined as the *ability* to do work. So, no, I do not think an ability is anything physical although it often enables the possessor to manifest in certain ways in the physical world. So there is a substantiality to the *self*, but it is not something physical.

And remember, all of the above is merely an attempt to identify what we are talking about when we refer to our *selves*. What you need to ask yourself is whether what I have said captures what you mean by your *self*, your *you*. If it does, wonderful! And if it doesn't, then try to come up with a definition that you think more accurately reflects what you mean by your *self*.

This subject may, at first, have struck the reader as obvious and a no-brainer. You can't even ask somebody the question without presuming that they have a self. We all experience our selves as the source of our decisions, choices, and inclinations as well as the locus of our experience. That which has, is consciously aware of, and interprets our experience. But you should know that there is a whole philosophical and religious tradition (Buddhism) which claims that there is **no self**. We'll talk about this more extensively in Ch. 7, below. But for here, suffice it to say that what they mean by this claim is not so easy to clarify or justify.

In any event, I just wanted the reader to know that there are a good many wise and serious people who actually do believe that there is **no self**. It's not a stupid or a silly claim. But it is certainly one which demands clarity and explanation since it *seems,* to virtually all of the rest of us, that each of us does indeed have or is a self.

And we are not yet done. There are still other characteristics involved in this notion of our *selves*.

2. As already mentioned, certainly **consciousness** is part of our self. And what's that? What's consciousness? Knowing what the word refers to is fairly easy. But defining it is a whole other matter. We might say, for example, that being conscious is being aware, being sensitive to, what is and what is happening around us. And this would involve some awareness of ourselves as subjects of experience. And that would, it seems, lead to a distinction between simply being conscious and being self-conscious. So far, in this little effort to pin down consciousness, so good. Most readers will readily recognize what is being talked about. We are conscious when we are *aware* of what is happening to us and of what we are doing at any moment. But *'aware'* and *'conscious'* are pretty much just synonyms, yes? Yes. Which points to what was said above: we readily *know* what we mean by consciousness, but defining it (without simply using synonyms) is a more difficult task. For now, however, we'll just go with, be satisfied with, that *knowing*. For the effort, at this point, is not so much to define consciousness but to agree that being conscious and having the ability to be both conscious and self-conscious, is indeed part of what we include in any notion of our *self*.

One last clarification on this topic of consciousness. Does anything that is conscious have a *self*? Does a worm have a self?

A dog? A porpoise? An elephant? Are any of those animals *self*-conscious, aware of themselves as unique individuals? There seems to be some evidence that among the bigger-brained animals in this group, there is a degree of self-consciousness But we don't need to determine an answer to that question here. Our goal here is to satisfactorily describe or define what we mean by our *selves*. And I think we have done enough so that we can discuss it and be in agreement about what we are talking about.. Our *self* involves a conscious and a self-conscious entity which is a source of action and is described as having a personality (desires, inclinations, styles of behavior), and a character (habits of action) and which changes (develops?) over time but retains a discernible continuity through those changes.

> [An aside: how can we reconcile this definition/description of a *self* with our experience of friends and family who have experienced or are experiencing **dementia**, especially personality-altering dementia? Has their 'self' disappeared? Or is it rather an instance of their various abilities *to express* that self (speech, memory, mental acuity, . . .) have become damaged and therefore the person is no longer able to act *as themselves*? Or is this just a desperate attempt to save a *self* that is not composed of anything material or physical?]

3. Now that we have some idea of what we mean by our ***self*** and of the complications that idea involves, we can go on to consider another of the 'doors' our initial question opens. Can and does the *self,* as we have described it here, continue in **existence beyond the death of our body**?

Well, if it can, and if it does, then apparently there is some ***spiritual realm*** or ***reality.*** Some realm or reality which is not physical nor composed of anything physical nor dependent upon anything physical for its existence. And this would be so because we would be claiming that something exists even though it is not physical nor is it dependent upon anything physical. (The body and all its components having reverted to "dust" and eventually their last constituent atoms.) So that's a really big "if" – a lot would follow from any affirmative answer to that *"can* it?" and that *"does* it?" In addition to one's self, for example, there would and *could* be consciousness (without a brain) a God, angels, demons, and some form of afterlife.

Another question that is raised by this line of thought would be: could we ever *know* if this were the case? No doubt we can believe that it is, and many people do so. But does it have to remain in the realm of belief? Or is it something we could actually come to *know*? For now, I'll just raise the question. We'll try to deal with it more fully in Ch. 3.

4. Finally, the last subject area (and the most important?) that our original question opens is: if one's **self** does persist beyond the death of the body, does/should that affect how one lives now? And that, it seems, would depend on **whether what we do now affects in any way what happens to us after the death of our body**. If it does or can, then prudence alone would dictate that it *should* affect how we live and act now. (Assuming, of course, that we know (have some reasonable belief about) *how* the two are related; *how* whatever we do now will affect what happens to us, to our selves, after the death of our body.

Virtually all of the world's religions, e.g., believe that how we live now <u>will</u> affect what happens to us after the death of our bodies. They 'see' and describe that afterlife differently, of course, but all of them think there is some connection between how we live in the here and now and any afterlife we may experience. This fact, the fact that virtually all of the world's religions share this belief is not, by itself, a very strong argument to believe it yourself. But, generally speaking, most of those religions have *some* wisdom to offer us on how to live and what is so. Though we should not simply just take their word for it, neither should we dismiss their worldviews without a thought. Their agreement alone on this issue is provocative and possibly insightful.

5. Whoops! I misspoke above, when I said that "the last 'door'" was this one about how and whether any afterlife, if there is one, does/should affect how one lives now. There is another 'door' or subject that is opened by this whole discussion. The subject of **free will**. Do we have such? Are we able to analyze, reflect, consider options and alternative consequences and choose to act or not, or are we simply living out the chain of mechanical causes and effects that govern the operations of the physical world? If we are not free, as just described, then whether an afterlife *should* affect how we live in the here and now becomes moot. If we have no choice about how we act and live, then whatever afterlife there may be is pre-determined and there's nothing we can do about it.

Sooooo, that original question was a rich one indeed. It does raise many of the more important questions that people have struggled with over the centuries and even millennia. Whether there is a **self** and how it might best be described or characterized. What is **consciousness,** which seems to be a necessary component of any *self* we have/are, and is it wholly dependent upon the brain? Can and does any self **persist beyond the death of the body**? Indeed, **does *any* spiritual realm or reality actually exist**? Further, if there is a personal afterlife, **how is it affected,** if at all, **by how we live in the here and now**? And finally, <u>**are we**</u>, in fact, **free** to choose and to act in one way rather than another?

The rest of this book will be an attempt to say something intelligent and helpful about each of these topics.

Chapter Outline   **Chapter 2**

Does Anything *Spiritual* Exist?

The question is important because so much follows from an answer either way. . . .
What *exactly* are we talking about when we speak of the spiritual, or of anything spiritual?
(1) Start with something quite different from, *(totally other than?)*, **the material**.
   Matter (or the physical) has such characteristics as: shape, size, weight, color, density, . . .
   And the spiritual is then defined as something which is totally non-material or non-physical.
   Does such a thing make any sense? Is it imaginable? Is it conceivable?
   And its "plausibility" or not involves us in another word's meaning. The word 'exist'. **Meaning of 'exist'**. . . . .
One additional clarification is needed before we can proceed, viz. regarding
   The Subjective. Are such entities (thoughts, desires, beliefs, fears, hopes,. . .) *spiritual*? They could be called so, but there is a problem: viz., that (virtually) all of these subjective entities and experiences are, in our current state, seemingly dependent upon our having a body and a brain. And this leads us to the final criterion for something being 'spiritual' in the classical sense: that, in addition to not being material,

(2) **Nor is it *dependent upon*** the physical or material for its existence.
Putting it all together, then, what we have so far is: *the spiritual* refers to . . . .

(3) **The Spiritual and its relationship to consciousness**.
Will a definition of consciousness help us get any clarity? Let's try. . . . .
   These questions remain then: is consciousness itself something spiritual?
   Or, is anything spiritual also and thereby something conscious?

(4) **But wait!** There seems to be yet other alternatives to the matter-spirit dichotomy, viz. something like the **matter-energy equivalence** in Physics, $E = Mc^2$. And think also of the wave-particle **complementarity**. (Introduces a new theme in these essays: monism vs. dualism.)   (See Ch. 5)

(5) Finally, there is at least one more question about *the spiritual* which we need to consider. And that is whether we can determine *any* coherent meaning for our original question?

I think that we can, though becoming clear about what exactly that meaning is turned out to be more difficult than we might have first thought. But, it seems, there is enough clarity of meaning that it makes sense to ask the question that drives this Ch.

Chapter 2
The Spiritual

Does anything *spiritual* actually exist? <u>Is there</u> any *spiritual* realm or reality?

The question is important because so many important 'things' (entities, realities, substances?) are deemed to be such. E.g., God, one's soul or one's *self*, one's mind (and Mind), an afterlife (in many religious traditions), ... ("Important" at least in the lives of most persons-on-the-street. In their understanding of themselves, of life, and of 'what it's all about'. E.g., roughly 85% of the world's population claim to be members of some religion or other, and the swamping majority of religions believe in some form of spiritual reality or spiritual realm. Are they all misguided and simply wrong about that? Or do they have something important to tell us?)

Well then, the first thing it would seem that we need to do is to come to some agreed upon understanding of what exactly we are talking about when we speak of the spiritual, or of anything spiritual.

(1) And what first comes to mind when we consider this question is: the spiritual is something quite different from, totally other than?, the material. Matter (or the physical) has such characteristics as: spatial dimensions, shape, weight or mass, electrical charge, 'spin', and can (at least theoretically) be 'cut' or divided into parts. Some of these features, of course, are not at all obvious or clear at the sub-atomic or quantum level, but generally we seem in agreement about what constitutes something being material or physical. And the spiritual is then defined as something which is totally <u>non</u>-material or non-physical. Something which exists but has none of those material characteristics.

Does that make any sense? Is it even conceivable? That it *could be* the case certainly seems possible, whether or not it actually is the case is what we'll be looking at in more depth in the remainder of this chapter. ("Possible" because there is no contradiction in the very notion of something spiritual.)

But its "possibility" or not involves us in another word's meaning. **The word "exist"**. What do we mean if we say that the spiritual *exists* or that something spiritual *could exist*? I'm going to suggest that what we mean by it is something very similar to what we mean when we say that anything material exists. Namely, that the 'thing' in question, whether a mountain or a baseball, a mind or God, can have an effect outside of itself. Can have an effect on something other than itself.

> [Can have an effect or does have an effect? A reasonable question, but one I'm not going to deal with here because it will distract us from the main thrust of this chapter.]

There is one additional clarification needed before we can deal with our original question and this clarification deals with something which is both intimately familiar to us and is yet something which is easy to get confused about in this context. What I'm talking about here is: *the subjective*. I.e., those items or aspects of our experience which we have no doubt about, of which we would say with great confidence and even vehemence that they exist, but which do not have any of the usual physical characteristics noted above. I'm speaking here of our thoughts, beliefs, hopes, fears, imaginings, feelings, etc.. No weight, no shape, no color, not divisible, no gravitational impact, . . How should we think of these? Are they something *spiritual*?

Thoughts, beliefs, hopes, etc. could be called spiritual, but there is a problem. And that problem points us to one more and a very important aspect of what we usually mean by *the spiritual*. And that is that virtually all of these subjective entities / experiences are, at least as we experience them in the here and now, dependent upon our having a body and a brain. I don't want to say that they definitely <u>are</u> so dependent, but certainly as we usually experience them in our daily lives, they seem to be so. (The exceptions would be things like: memories of past lives, near death experiences, and out-of-body experiences. But these are not part of most people's daily lives or experiences, so I'll bracket them off to the side for now.)

(2) And this leads us to the final criterion for something's being 'spiritual'. That it **not be dependent upon** the physical or material **for its existence**. Putting it all together, then, what we now have is: *the spiritual* refers to something which is not material or physical and neither is it dependent upon anything material for its existence, and yet it does *exist*, it <u>can</u> have an effect outside of itself. And since the subjective, as we experience it, does *seem* dependent upon something(s) material (the brain, e.g.), the *spiritual* we are inquiring about will, at least for now, also be considered to be something other than, something over and above the purely subjective. Does any such 'thing' exist?

> Note that whether the subjective is actually other than the spiritual would be something to be determined. Maybe those thoughts, beliefs, hopes, fears, imaginings, feelings, etc. are, in fact, *spiritual* entities. Could something without

either a brain or a body have such? We are not rejecting this possibility out-of-hand by drawing this distinction between the spiritual and the subjective, but only saying that <u>as we now experience things</u> and understand what we experience, thoughts, feeling, etc.. do seem dependent upon our having a brain and a body.

Well, then, have we arrived at an understanding of <u>what</u> we (and of what most people) <u>mean by</u> the *spiritual*? Something which is neither material nor dependent upon the material for its existence and yet which can have an effect outside of itself (= does actually *exist*).

And remember, we have *not* yet *argued* that something spiritual <u>does</u> exist. All we have done so far is to try to come to agreement about what exactly we are talking about, about what exactly the question heading this chapter is asking.

(3) But, (isn't there *always* a "but"!) there is at least one more feature of *the spiritual* which we need to consider. And that is **its relationship to consciousness**. Is anything spiritual also something conscious? Does anything conscious have something spiritual 'in' it? Can there be an unconscious but spiritual reality? Are the two terms synonymous? Consciousness is something spiritual or it simply <u>is</u> the spiritual? Is it the case that anything being spiritual <u>is the same as</u> being conscious **or** anything spiritual <u>is also</u> conscious?

Whew! Lots of possibilities. What exactly is the relationship between consciousness and the spiritual? And again, is being conscious dependent upon the body or the brain? Do we have any evidence one way or the other? (See Ch. 3)

Will a definition of consciousness help us get any clarity on this? Let's try. Consciousness seems to mean or refer to our (anything's) <u>ability</u> to be aware and its actually <u>being aware of itself as a source of activity and of receiving such activity from</u> others. An awareness of one's place and functions in a world of inter-connections or inter-relationships.

Hmmmm. As just stated, we actually have two 'things' being spoken of. Awareness and <u>Self</u>-awareness. Can one be conscious without also being self-conscious? I would think that one can. It seems to me, e.g., that a worm may well be conscious or aware of its surroundings without having any sense of itself as a separate entity. On such an analysis, consciousness/awareness and self-consciousness or self-awareness are distinguishable and the second (self-consciousness) would be seen as a higher degree or instance of simple consciousness.

OK, but does that add any light to our question about the relationship between the spiritual and consciousness? I don't see that it does. The questions remain: is consciousness itself something spiritual? And is anything spiritual also and thereby something conscious?

(4) And as if that's not enough of a puzzle, it turns out that there are still other possibilities that maybe we should take into account. Consider, e.g., something like $E = Mc^2$. I.e. the possibility that the spiritual is a kind of transformation of/on the physical or vice versa.

And there is also the whole notion of *complementarity* (particle and wave, e.g.). *Looked at in one way*, it's a particle (something physical); but looked at in another way, it's a wave (something non physical). Looked at in one way, it is dependent upon the physical, but looked at in another way, it neither is nor is it dependent upon the physical.

(5) Well then, are we reduced to either incoherence or silence when it comes to speaking of the *spiritual*, or of something being *spiritual*? I think not. We may not be able to come up with an exact definition of the spiritual, and yet we are able to speak intelligibly about it. We can 'get at it' in various ways that both pick out what we are talking about and say enough intelligible about it so that whomever we are talking with knows of which we speak, knows what we are referring to. (And again, please note that being able to talk about it does not, by itself, prove or show that it actually does exist as described.) Consider as an example of just such a situation, Richard Feynman's comment on **energy**:

"It is important to realize that in physics today, we have no knowledge of what energy is."

> [Richard Feynman was an American theoretical physicist, known for his work in the path integral formulation of quantum mechanics, the theory of quantum electrodynamics, the physics of the superfluidity of supercooled liquid helium, as well as his work in particle physics for which he proposed the parton model. For contributions to the development of quantum electrodynamics, Feynman received the Nobel Prize in Physics in 1965 jointly with Julian Schwinger and Shin'ichiro Tomonaga. . . . .
>
> During his lifetime, Feynman became one of the best-known scientists in the world. In a 1999 poll of 130 leading

> physicists worldwide by the British journal Physics World, he was ranked the seventh-greatest physicist *of all time!*" (emph. mine)
> https://en.wikipedia.org/wiki/Richard_Feynman]

And yet physicists talk about energy all the time and communicate well about it. We, they, *know* what they are referring to and we have some ideas about what it involves even if we can't give an exhaustive and universally accepted definition of exactly what it is. I think the *spiritual* is similar. We've come close to saying what it is and all that it is (above), but there are still puzzles and questions about it. Nevertheless, we can speak meaningfully with each other about it, and that's what we'll attempt to do in the remainder of this book.

The categories we use to describe and explain our every day experience become increasingly inadequate as we move further away from that every day experience, whether that is done via science or mysticism.

In sum, and where we are now on the subject, the *spiritual* will be understood to be something which is neither physical nor dependent upon the physical for its existence (and therefore something which is not composed or has no parts), but yet something which does *exist* (can affect 'things' outside of/other than itself); something which either is conscious (and <u>self</u>-conscious) or is consciousness itself; and is something which is intimately related to (fundamentally characteristic of) our *selves*, our *souls*, our *'hearts'* and *minds*.

Chapter Outline   **Chapter 3**   (See also Bk. 4, Ch's. 2 & 4)

What are you willing to accept as evidence for or against a claim about the spiritual?

An absolutely pivotal question. Perhaps, even, *the most determinative* for answering the question of Ch. 2. (A look back at Ch. 2, for meanings.)

History, Experience and Argument

1. <u>History</u>: e.g., 4,000 years of the world's religions . . . . ; "The Great Chain of Being" . . . ;

2. <u>Personal Experience</u>: **Events which** *seem to* **defy materialistic explanations and which point to a spiritual realm. E.g., resurrection; miracles; memories of past lives; consciousness without brain activity (OBE's and NDE's); mystical and psychedelic experiences;**   See also, Bk. 1, Ch. 4
   <u>Counter</u> *arguments* to "Personal Experience": "*seem to,*" but really don't. We just don't yet know what the *physical* causes of these are. (But note the question-begging assumption behind this objection.)
   Or, we do know what the physical cause is (in the case of psychedelics, e.g.) but not the validity of the experience.

3. **The effect(s) your experience(s) of the spiritual can have on you. . . .**
   <u>Counter</u> *argument*: but, is it the spiritual itself or your beliefs about it having those effects? Compare: the placebo effect.
   <u>Falsification experience(s)</u>: E.g., death followed by no consciousness whatever. But what about *now*?? Can you think of any you could have *now*? (**Problem of Evil.**)

4. <u>Argument(s)</u>. **for and against.**   (See also Bk. 3, Ch. on Apologetics)
Taking God as an example of something spiritual. (If God exists, then something spiritual exists.)
    Some <u>arguments</u> *for*: Cardinal Newman's argument.
                  The Kalam cosmological argument.
                  An argument from contingency. (E.g. *Udana* 8.3)

    Some <u>arguments</u> *against*:   Impossible to falsify it *now*.
                             The Problem of Evil.
                          ✓ The argument from science, (and its fatal flaw).
So, what are *you* willing to accept as evidence for or against the claim that something spiritual exists?

Chapter 3
What are you willing to accept as evidence either for or against the claim that there is a spiritual (metaphysical?) realm or reality?

The first thing to note is what a pivotal question this is. If the issue under consideration (in our case, whether there is any spiritual realm or reality) is a real question, a question that has an answer one way or the other, and you're not going to settle the issue merely by a coin flip, then there must be something on which you're going to base your answer. That 'something' is what is usually referred to as the evidence in support of whatever answer you give. And we (including you) judge the likelihood of your answer being true based on the evidence you refer to in order to support your position. Typically, we look to such aspects of the evidence as: if the evidence is true, does it in fact support the position you want to hold? And what is (are) the source(s) for the evidence you are depending on? How informed, trustworthy, dependable, consistent, etc. are they (whether they are live persons or data). And is the reasoning of your argument connecting the evidence to the conclusion you hold, valid? Does it hide any errors of logic?

So, in this case, what evidence is there or, more to the point, <u>what evidence are you willing to accept</u>, for the claim that there is some spiritual realm or reality. (For the meaning of these terms, refer to the previous chapter.)

I want to look at three different kinds of evidence that have been depended upon in the past and currently in coming to a judgment about the spiritual: **history**, **experience** and **argument**. Each of them has its own benefits and difficulties. And (spoiler alert) I can guarantee that no one of them, nor all of them taken together, is/are going to convince everyone of what to believe. Nevertheless, I do hope that our discussion will add some light to your own musings on this topic.

(1) What do I mean by **the "history"** of this notion of a spiritual realm or a spiritual reality? I will focus on two things in speaking of this history: the various religions of the world and something called "the great chain of being."

With respect to the first, **the world's religions**: all of the world's major religions profess to believe / think that <u>there is</u> such a thing as a spiritual reality or a spiritual realm. Indeed, their whole purpose seems to be to help us understand and to tell us how to navigate in our relationship with this spiritual reality or realm. Currently, about 85% of the world's population professes belief in one or other of these religions. The swamping majority of that 85% would be constituted by Christianity, Islam, Hinduism, Buddhism, Judaism and the various Folk religions.

> (Another aspect of this history, but one I'll postpone looking at until we get to the experience component later in this chapter, is the fact of (or at least the claims about) mystical experiences had by the monks, mendicants, gurus, lamas, hermits, ascetics, Sufis and other devotees of these religions *over the centuries*. Despite the many differences in doctrine and practice between these various religions, they all seem to have within them devotees who claim to have <u>actually experienced</u> some spiritual realm or reality.)

And I suspect that as we go back in time and history, an even greater percentage of the world's population would profess to believe in some religion or other and that most of those religions would be like the big five noted above in that they also would have as a foundational belief that something spiritual, some spiritual realm or reality does exist.

Some or many of you may be saying to yourselves about now: "who cares about this history??!" Humans have believed all sorts of things over the years which we now know to be false, and the fact that they may have believed them for long periods of time does not necessarily add any authority or probability to the claim(s) professed. And you would be right, of course. On the other hand, whether it's certain plants having particular medicinal qualities or close, extended families being important for many things important to humans, to the personal qualities that make for good character and the importance of the latter, these long held and virtually universal beliefs <u>do acquire *some* authority</u> if for no other reason than that they do seem to express functionally helpful world views for the people who hold them. "Functionally helpful" to the people who hold them may not be equivalent to nor lead to: <u>is true</u>. But, it seems to me, it is a fact worth considering.

But you would be right if you were to react to this fact by saying: "So what? They might *believe* it but they could be wrong about it too." Yes indeed, they could. Nevertheless I do think it shows us a couple of important points. **The first** is that the notion of a spiritual realm or reality, of a realm or reality that is other than or outside of the physical reality within which we live and move and have our being, has a loooong history among humans and, seemingly, responds to either an innate human need or some equally innate human impulse or instinct. In doing so, does such a realm or reality represent a genuine correlate of our being? Are our instincts in this case, however inchoate and descriptively different they may be over cultures and time, revelatory? Or, is the human instinct to believe such nothing more than the desperate grasping of frightened beings in the face of the immense unknowns of the world and universe?

And **a second** point this history of religion shows us is that the very notion of a spiritual realm or reality has <u>not</u> been shown to be incoherent. Whether something spiritual <u>does</u> exist or not is certainly, and has been, disputed. Whether such *could* exist is not equally disputed. The issue there, rather, has to do with the leading question of this chapter: <u>what would you accept as evidence for or against the claim</u> that anything spiritual, any spiritual realm or reality, actually exists?

So, the first evidence of history is simply the numerous religions that have and do exist among human kind; religions which have as a (the?) essential part of their belief systems that something spiritual, some spiritual realm or reality exists. And this history stretches back roughly 2500 years from our current time. And further, though many of the adherents of these religions over the ages have been simple, uneducated folk, not all of them have been so. In a number of these religions, there were (and are) some very bright, highly educated, thoughtful persons who hold these beliefs about a spiritual realm or reality. Such beliefs are evidently <u>not</u> absurd, silly or obviously false.

The second subject I want to talk about **with regard to history** offering *some* evidence for the existence of a spiritual reality or spiritual realm has to do with what has been called **"The Great Chain of Being"**. I think this phrase itself may have been coined by

Arthur Lovejoy back in the 1930's, but the concept it refers to has been around at least since Plato (in the West).

The basic idea in this notion or theory is that there are different levels of existence. That a rock, e.g., exists in a way that is inferior to (has less *be-ing* than) a plant. And a plant exists in a way that is inferior to (has less *be-ing* than) an animal. And so on up a chain of be-ing at which, on each subsequent step up the chain, what exists on that step or that level somehow exists more fully than whatever exists on the steps below it. And that "somehow exists more fully" is usually filled in by referring to abilities that each subsequent step's inhabitors have that the 'lower' step's inhabitors don't have. E.g. life, physical movement, consciousness, self-consciousness, simple thought, language, aesthetic sensibility and creativity, conceptual thinking, . . . And at the higher end of such a chain of be-ing would be the spiritual. 'Things' that exist on a spiritual plane or in a spiritual way. They would have all the abilities of whatever exists on the steps below them, but they would have additional abilities (and potentialities) that those on the lower steps do not have. Thus, on those higher steps would be entities such as angels (and demons) and, ultimately, God (if such exists).

So the generating idea behind this notion of a chain of being seems pretty clear and obvious. A tree certainly does seem to exist on a level or in a way/s that a rock does not exist. And similarly so between a tree and your dog, e.g.. And so on up the chain. But when we get to something purely spiritual as distinct from something that is a combination of the physical and the 'spiritual' (human beings, e.g.), we may balk. Yes, the notion of a purely spiritual reality or realm does fall within such a hierarchy, but perhaps at that level it is *just* a notion, merely <u>an idea of</u> *a possible* reality.

And again, the objector may be right about this. I raised this notion of The Great Chain of Being not as any proof for the existence of a spiritual realm or reality, but rather as an instance of where **history** might be turned to in support of such a notion. It (the Great Chain of Being) has been around in human thought for a long period of time. That longevity and persistence may well be, it seems to me, not only indicative, it may also be revelatory.

(2) The next kind of evidence I want to consider is **personal experience**. The first such relates to our, virtually all humans', experience of the numinous and of morality. And here I'll just refer the reader to some passages in C. S. Lewis's little book titled: *The Problem of Pain*, pp. 19-23. The key, for our purposes, is his argument that though these experiences are and have been universal throughout the history of man, their cause cannot be traced back to the physical elements of our lives.

> "When man passes from physical fear to dread and awe [the numinous], he makes a sheer jump, and apprehends something which could never be given, as danger is, by the physical facts and logical deduction from them." (p. 20) And

> "All the human beings that history has heard of acknowledge some kind of morality; that is, they feel towards certain proposed actions the experiences expressed by the words "I ought" or "I ought not." These experiences resemble awe in one respect, namely that they cannot be logically deduced from the environment and physical experiences of the man who undergoes them. . . . . And, once again, attempts to resolve the moral experience into something else always presuppose the very thing they are trying to

> explain– as when a famous psychoanalyst deduces it from prehistoric parricide. If the parricide produced a sense of guilt, that was because men felt that they ought not to have committed it: if they did not so feel, it could produce no sense of guilt. Morality, like numinous awe, is a jump; in it man goes beyond anything that can be "given" in the facts of experience." (Ibid. p. 21)

Secondly, some people have claimed, over the centuries of human life on earth, that they have actually experienced some kind of spiritual reality or a spiritual realm. This experience ranges from simple visions of something that or someone who is not physical, to an experience of some ultimate reality, something that exists but is, or appears to them to be, significantly different from anything and everything else they have ever experienced in their lives.

Another feature of these kinds of experiences is that it usually occurs to someone who has or is taking steps to prepare for it or to enable it to occur. Thus the most common subject of these experiences has usually been religious devotees of various stripes, from Christian, Buddhist and Hindu monks and hermits to Islamic Sufis, Jewish Kabbalists, and other members of mystical traditions. (This fact, of course, can be seen as undermining their claim(s). Following the dictum of: "you 'see' what you expect to 'see'," one could easily doubt or question whether what they have experienced is actually as they have interpreted it to be.)

But there are enough other kinds of experience, <u>non-mystical</u> kinds, which seem to point to a spiritual realm or reality that it behooves us, I think, to pay some attention to this kind of evidence. Here, I am thinking of such things as Christ's resurrection (assuming it occurred), miracles, memories of past lives[1], consciousness without any detectable brain activity, near death experiences (NDEs)[2], out-of-body experiences (OBEs), and more recently the many experiences had by people under the influence of psychedelics or entheogens. All of these point in the direction of: there is more to existence and existing than what is involved in our purely physical, bodily, existence. There does seem to be something we might call a spiritual reality or a spiritual realm or way of existing. And occasionally, people seem able to tap into this reality.[3]

The most usual counter to this line of thinking is that these various **experiences** may *seem to* rely on or need some form of spiritual realm or reality to explain them but that assumption is merely an artifact of our own lack of knowledge. That really, it's just a matter of our not yet knowing *how* to explain these experiences without recourse to some spiritual reality or realm, but that there is such an explanation. However, as we'll see later in this chapter, this retort is itself usually based on a question-begging assumption and to that extent and for that reason, must be rejected.

(3) A corollary, if you will, of this class of evidence for the existence of a spiritual reality or realm, is **the effect such experiences have on their subjects**. Here, it is argued, that the experience must be real because it often has such life-altering effects on the person

---

[1] Cf. the extensive research of Dr. Ian Stevenson at Univ. of Virginia's Medical School, Division of Perceptual Studies.

[2] Cf. the research of Dr. Bruce Greyson also at UVA's Division of Perceptual Studies, and his book: *After*

[3] A more recent and very extensive taxonomy and discussion of the different kinds of spiritual experience can be found in *The Varieties of Spiritual Experience* by David Yaden and Andrew Newberg.

who claims to have had the experience. Those effects range from a significantly different view of the world, of what exists, to how they should lead their lives going forward. The vision that supposedly happened to St. Paul on the road to Damascus and its subsequent effect on his life are a classic example of this kind of thing.

The counter to this line of reasoning, however, is: 'ahh, but is it the experience itself which has had these life-altering effects or the person's *belief* in *their interpretation of* that experience which is actually having the cited effects?' And if it's just their *belief* that is the cause, then we really have no evidence about the experience itself. I have no idea how to settle this issue. But it does raise a really, really important point that we'll deal with in chapter 4, viz. the issue that **any experience involves an interpretation** of what it is an experience of and of what has caused the experience.

Finally, we come to an apparently strong counter-argument that falls within this category of **experience**. What I am thinking of here is the notion of *falsification*. This is the notion, commonly held in the sciences, that any claim is (empirically) meaningful and true only if there is some state of affairs which would count against its being true. If there is not, then the claim being made cannot be tested and thus cannot be shown to be true. (And beyond that, is it even meaningful?) E.g., the theory of gravity (as Newton conceived of it) claims that objects heavier than air would fall toward the earth if left unsupported. So this claim would be shown to be false if some heavier-than-air objects when left unsupported did not fall toward the earth. The claim is subject to falsification and therefore is a meaningful claim, is a claim that can be shown to be true or false. (More precisely: it is subject to *empirical* falsification and therefore is an *empirically* meaningful claim.)

But note that this test was originally meant as a test for empirical claims, i.e. claims that the physical sciences deal with. Thus "state of affairs" here is interpreted to mean some *empirical* state of affairs, some state of affairs that is susceptible of sensory experience.

Nevertheless, it seems natural enough to think that something like it must be so for claims of any sort. E.g. claims even about some spiritual realm or reality. If such claims are true, there must be *some* state of affairs that would count against them even if it is not an empirical state of affairs. There must be some state of affairs such that, if it existed, the claim in question would not be true.

Well then, is this the case for claims about a spiritual realm or reality? Of course it is, *but* we may not be able to access those states of affairs in the here-and-now. Thus, e.g., any claim about our having immortal souls would be shown to be false if no conscious self existed after the death of our body. Unfortunately, we can't test that possibility in any way that we could show to others in the here-and-now. (Discounting any truth to seances.) But that doesn't mean it isn't true or even that it isn't meaningful. It only means that it is not currently testable in any way that can be shown to others.

There is a possible exception to this conclusion about not being able to test any claim about a spiritual realm or reality, and it's a very, very strong move based on falsification. (Though its strength may be more psychological than logical.) And that is what has come to be called **the problem of evil.**

We'll speak more about this later in this chapter (under Arguments), but to tie it in with what we have been saying here about falsification, it would go like this: there is a state of affairs which, if it existed, would falsify a particular (but widely believed) spiritual claim. That widely believed spiritual claim is that there is a God who is all-powerful, all-knowing and all-good. And the state of affairs that would, if it existed, be in_compatible with such a claim is one in which innocent people were caused to suffer greatly. But, the argument goes, that is exactly the state of affairs that obtains in the world we inhabit, many innocent people suffer greatly from disease, from accidents, from wars, from starvation. So there cannot be an all-powerful, all-knowing and an all-good God since if He were all-good He would not want innocent people to suffer and if He were all-powerful, He could keep that from happening. A powerful argument indeed and one that has proven to be perhaps *the* most influential in determining whether people believe in a God. We'll deal with this argument more fully under the section (below) on arguments.

(4) We've said a bit about history and personal experience. Now, we'll look at **arguments** as ways of providing evidence for the existence of a spiritual realm or reality. I'll first take a look at three different arguments **for** the existence of a spiritual realm or reality. (Most (all?) are arguments for the existence of God or of an ultimate reality, with the obvious connection that if such a being exists, then something spiritual exists.)

The first of these arguments that I want to present is also, I think, the simplest and most direct. (And throughout, I'll present these arguments in my words, not those of the originators. Any failure to represent them fully or adequately is all mine.)

Cardinal John Henry Newman's argument:

If something exists now, then something must always have existed.
(Because you can't get something from nothing.)
So, we have a choice, either that "something that has always existed" is the matter-energy dyad or it is intelligence.
Intelligence seems the much more likely option to me (Newman),
So, that which has always existed is (infinite) intelligence (or God).
(On this latter equivalence, consider also

Freeman Dyson: "God is what mind becomes when it has passed beyond the scale of our comprehension."

Or Einstein's: "It is enough for me to contemplate the mystery of conscious life perpetuating itself through all eternity, to reflect upon the marvelous structure of the universe which we dimly perceive, and to try humbly to comprehend an infinitesimal part of *the intelligence manifested in nature.*"   (emph. mine)

One of the things I like about this argument is that it concludes with a choice rather than some apodictic statement. In doing so, Newman seems to be acknowledging that it's not possible *to force* anyone to accept that God exists by argument and logic alone. And I think he is right about that. Any argument provides some evidence pro or con, but there are always ways to avoid accepting the conclusion. It's one of the reasons I phrased the heading for this chapter as I have. What *evidence* would you accept either for or against the claim that something spiritual, some spiritual realm or reality, exists? What evidence would you accept <u>as counting</u> either <u>for or against</u> such a claim?

The next two arguments are considerably more complex and difficult, but I'll try to present them in as straight-forward and clear a fashion as I can. Hopefully without over simplifying them. And the question to ask yourself, when all is said and done, is: do either (or both) of them give you what you would consider to be *evidence* for the conclusion that something spiritual actually does exist?

The Cosmological Argument –

This argument has a looooong and respected, and debated, history. Parts of it can be traced back to Aristotle and books and books upon books have been written about it. So I hope the reader will understand and be tolerant of the very shortened version and commentary that I'll be giving it in this book.

For fuller treatments, I can recommend as starting points the following: <u>https://plato.stanford.edu/entries/cosmological-argument/</u> and on a particular version of it, <u>https://en.wikipedia.org/wiki/Kalam cosmological argument</u>.

Essentially, this argument is based on the impossibility of an actual infinite regress. I.e. that the universe, the cosmos, everything material that exists, cannot always have existed. Aristotle's reason for thinking this was, as I recall, that if you could go back infinitely in time, then you could never get to here. But, obviously, we (the cosmos) has gotten to here, so there must have been a beginning at some point. I'll leave it to the reader to determine whether Aristotle's argument succeeds.

The argument then goes: whatever has begun to exist, must have a cause for its beginning. (Because you can't get something from nothing.) The physical universe, the cosmos, began to exist. So there must be a cause for its beginning to exist. And that cause must be something which has always existed (otherwise, it would have to have a cause for its existence). In fact, it must be something which cannot not exist. Thus it cannot be part of the cosmos itself since then it would be something which has begun, at some point in time, to exist. Such a being, such an entity, one that cannot not exist or one that exists necessarily, is what most people refer to as God. And that being which is not part of the physical universe or cosmos, is neither composed nor contingent and thus is something spiritual.

As mentioned above, this argument has a looooong and a debated history. There are numerous places where philosophers and theologians have attacked it and where philosophers and theologians have, in response, defended it. My presentation of it, above, is by no means exhaustive. Rather, it's only meant to give the reader some idea of what the argument says and what it involves. The point being that arguments are another way which people have used or depended upon for evidence of there being a spiritual realm or reality.

The argument from contingency –

Another such argument is what may be called the argument from contingency. This one, like the former cosmological argument, is a fairly difficult argument to follow, but, again, I'll try to simplify it (hopefully without losing any logical rigor it might have).

The essence of this argument is that if something is contingent, then it can go out of existence. And we must distinguish here between "go out of existence" as what it is, from go out of existence entirely. We might call the first, to go out of existence formally and the second, to go out of existence radically. An example of the first would be a wooden table which is reduced to chunks of wood and splinters. When that is done, the table no longer exists, but its constituents still do exist. Or, something might "go out of existence" entirely or radically; i.e. not only does its current form change, but also none of its constituent parts remain in existence *in any form*. An example of this latter may be when matter encounters anti-matter. It is my understanding that when this happens, both are completely annihilated. The argument from contingency which we are focused on here concerns this latter kind of contingency, radical contingency.

Now, the argument goes: if everything (the entire cosmos) were *radically* contingent, then it is possible that there be a time when nothing at all exists. But if there were ever a (past) time when absolutely nothing existed, then nothing would exist now. (Because, again, you can't get something from nothing.) But something does exist now. So there must never have been a time when absolutely nothing existed. (Since, in infinite time, all possibilities would, eventually, come to exist, if everything were contingent there would have been a time when nothing existed.) Thus, it must be the case that there is something which cannot go out of existence, or is not contingent. The opposite of being contingent is to be necessary, to be something which cannot not exist. So there must be something which exists necessarily. And that something is what we usually call God. (And if such a thing exists, then there is something which is spiritual.)

Unfortunately, (for him or her who believes in the spiritual) there are a couple of weak spots in this argument. The first is that one could simply counter-argue that there has not yet been infinite time. And if that's the case, then we can't say whether everything is radically contingent. Alternatively, one could question whether in infinite time, all possibilities would come to exist as is required by the original argument. I don't see why that would have to be the case.

So, there are arguments which might be turned to as evidence *for* the claim that something spiritual exists. But none of them seem airtight or impervious to counter-argument. And maybe that's the best one can do. I.e., here is something which may be taken *as evidence for* the claim in question, but it is not proof.

But can the same be said about any **arguments against the claim** that something spiritual, some spiritual realm or reality, exists? I'll take a brief look at three such arguments against. One I've already dealt with, one has been mentioned and one is new.

The argument I've already dealt with is that which deals with falsification. The argument was: if there is no state-of-affairs which would count against the claim that something spiritual exists, then the claim itself is meaningless. But the argument was defeated by pointing out that there are indeed states-of-affairs which would count against such a claim. E.g., the state of affairs in which nothing spiritual exists. We may not be able, in the here and now, to test whether such a state-of-affairs exists, but it certainly could exist and may even be susceptible to experiential testing (though not empirical testing). For example, you are dying and as your consciousness fades, it becomes crystal clear to you that you will never experience any subsequent conscious state.

The argument I've already mentioned is that based on the problem of evil (see above, p. 28). This is a very, very powerful argument. Certainly, one which is psychologically and emotionally very powerful. In fact, there may not be any other argument which has convinced more people of the correctness of their position that no such being as an all powerful and all good God exists. And note that in this instance, I am assuming that if God exists, then *something spiritual* exists.

Again, and briefly, the argument goes: if God is all-good, He/She/It would not want pain and suffering to befall innocent people. And if God is all-powerful, He/She/It could ensure that such did not happen. But such does happen, from disease, accidents, floods, fires, wars, birth defects, etc., etc.! So, such a God (an all-powerful and an all good God) must not exist. (And some modern philosophers have even argued that it would be a logical contradiction to claim that such a God exists.)

As you might expect, other philosophers and theologians have put forth arguments designed to show that this argument fails in its purpose. I.e. it does not prove that such a God does not or cannot exist. One such counter argument, one targeted to respond to the claimed logical impossibility of there being such an all-good and all-powerful God co-existing with the suffering of the innocent, is this: it is not incompatible for an all-good and an all-powerful God to exist in the presence of the suffering of the innocent just in case that suffering is *a necessary condition for* the existence of some good which is at least as great as the suffering is evil. This counter argument shares the same force as does the argument that God's inability to square the circle does not show that He/She/It is not all-powerful.

Logically, this argument passes muster; but psychologically and emotionally, and at first glance, it fails miserably. Which is probably one reason the author(s) of Job, didn't use it. Instead, they simply had God say the equivalent of: 'who are you (Job) to question the ways of God??!' Implying that God has His/Her/Its reasons for what happens and because of those reasons, the presence of innocent suffering does not count against the existence of an all-powerful and an all-good God.

And finally, **the argument from science against there being anything spiritual**, any spiritual realm or reality, where that is understood to mean a realm or a reality which is in no way physical or material nor is it dependent upon anything material for its existence, and yet which does exist.

The argument goes something like this: 'I know what science (currently) tells us. The universe, the cosmos, is expanding and apparently at an increasing rate. It is not going to reverse that expansion and ultimately collapse back in on itself. (The existence of the universe is not, therefore, cyclical.) Rather, and eventually, it is going to end up with all of its energy expended so that all that is left is an immensity of cold, dead cinders. (Ice in Robert Frost's wonderful little poem: *Fire and Ice*.) So that is what exists and that is all that exists. There is nothing like any spiritual realm or reality. Science tells us so.'

I have encountered this argument many, many times in my conversations with people about this topic. It does not have the psychological and emotional impact of the argument based on the problem of evil, but in our (Western) society today,– science driven and based as it is– it appears to have almost unquestioned standing.

The problem is, this argument **begs the question**! I.e. it assumes at the outset the very answer it was meant to investigate and show to be true or not. In this case, does what the empirical sciences study exhaust what can and does exist? You can't just assume that it does. You have to show or prove that it does. But if you restrict what can and does exist to only those things which are susceptible of empirical investigation, then you have merely stipulated an answer to this question without really investigating it.

Put another way, note the dilemma: Does anything spiritual exist? What would you accept as evidence that something spiritual exists? Ans.: Only something empirical. Sooooo, the only evidence you would accept that something non-empirical exists is something empirical. I.e., you have determined that nothing non-empirical *can* exist without appealing to any evidence to that effect, but only to a dogma that only something empirical can exist.

And that is exactly why the question that drives this chapter is so important: what would you accept as evidence for or against any particular position? If there is no evidence either way that you would accept, that you would base your judgment on, then your position is merely an unquestioned and apparently unquestionable dogma that you adhere to. (The definition of "closed minded".) And if there is only one kind of evidence that you would accept and that kind of evidence itself determines the answer one way or the other, then, again, you are adopting an answer before and irrespective of any countervailing evidence. I.e., you are begging the question. Either of these are ways one should strive to avoid.

****

* An example of **a transcendent experience** is beautifully described by a clergyman in William James's book: *Varieties of Religious Experience* (1902):

> "I remember the night, and almost the very spot on the hilltop, where my soul opened out, as it were, into the Infinite, and there was a rushing together of two worlds, the inner and the outer. It was deep calling unto deep– the deep that my own struggle had opened up within being answered by the unfathomable deep without, reaching beyond the stars. I stood alone with Him who had made me, and all the beauty of the world, and love, and sorrow, and even temptation. I did not seek Him, but felt the perfect union of my spirit with His . . . Since that time no discussion that I have heard of the proofs of God's existence has been able to shake my faith. Having once felt the presence of God's spirit, I have never lost it again for long. My most assuring evidence of his existence is deeply rooted in that hour of vision, in the memory of that supreme experience."

Chapter Outline   **Chapter 4**

Any and all experience involves an interpretation.

1. **Why it's important.**
If experience is depended upon (see Ch. 3) as a way of getting an answer to the question of Ch. 2,
any gap between having an experience and *interpreting* it to be an experience of...?
  or *knowing* that it is an experience of.....?
introduces the possibility of error, of <u>mis</u>interpreting your experience.

2. **Additional reasons for thinking the interpretation and the experience are distinct.**
<u>If no gap</u> between having the experience and *knowing* that it is an experience of _____.
  a.) Anyone who has the experience could not be wrong about what it was an experience of.
  b.) Anyone who has the experience would come away from the experience in agreement with anyone else who had *the same* experience as to what it was an experience of.
  (Problem with "the same" experience.)
But, from the mundane to the exotic, has this a.) & b.)] *ever* been so?
If not, we may conclude that <u>there is</u> a gap. (*Logically*, yes, but *as experienced?*)
And if a gap, then there is the possibility of a misinterpretation, or mis-identification.
  (And if no gap, then "learning from experience" would not be possible!)
So, it seems to be the case that with any experience we have, we also (and simultaneously?) **interpret** that experience? I.e., we make a judgment about
  1. what the experience is "of", or *what* it is we are experiencing. And usually, closely attached in time to that interpretation, is another:
  2. about <u>what is causing that experience</u>....
Examples....

3. **Other conclusions that can be drawn from the fact that: all experience involves an interpretation.**
   - The experience is not the same thing as the experien<u>cer</u> (whoever is doing the *interpretation*).
   - Dualism seems implied by the experience / experiencer distinction. See Ch. 5
   - "Peer review" has a place in and plays the same role in interpreting a spiritual experience as it does in interpreting scientific experiments.

4. **Does this possibility of error mean that experience can no longer be taken as evidence for the claim that something spiritual, some spiritual realm or reality, exists?**

Chapter 4
The Interpretation Of Any Experience

This is, I think, a fascinating subject and one with far reaching consequences. See what you think after reading what follows.

1. Why it's important.

We pick up, here, from Ch. 3 where we talked about experience as one kind of evidence that people might rely on to come to a conclusion about whether or not any spiritual realm or reality actually exists. The kinds of experiences we mentioned in that regard ranged from the witnesses to Christ's resurrection or to other miracles, to St. Paul's reporting of his experience on the road to Damascus, to mystical or mystical-like experiences had by saints in various religious traditions as well as by NDEs, OBEs, and memories of past lives to, finally, users of psychedelic drugs (sometimes referred to as entheogens) whether in a clinical setting or in traditional ceremonial contexts. In all of these cases, those involved came away with the conviction that what they experienced was real (actually exists), was revelatory (revealed something important about the way things are), and that it involved or revealed some sort of spiritual reality. And we want to now ask: how dependable are these reports of experiences?

Assuming that the people involved are sane, trying to be honest and have no hidden agenda, we can take it that they certainly had *some* experience and one which they have interpreted as being an experience of _____. And it's that last part "one which they have **interpreted** as being . . ." that opens the doors of inquiry and doubt. There's a gap between having the experience and judging/interpreting what the experience is of. Does the experience reveal something real and independent of us, the experiencer, e.g., or is it simply an awareness on our part caused by some physical or chemical event in our brain and neither indicating nor supporting *any* judgment about something outside of / independent of our brain? Are our brain and our consciousness acting as conduits, <u>windows</u> if you will, onto something other than themselves, or are they all that's there, simply <u>a screen</u>, the only thing happening? A moderate realism or a radical solipsism?

Consider an example, two actually. Imagine yourself on a beautiful clear Fall day looking at a far hillside that is covered in Aspen trees all of which have changed into their golden yellow Fall colors. It's gorgeous and stunning to the eye. (Exper. #1) Now imagine yourself in that same geographic and temporal position observing the same Aspen covered hillside, but having taken a moderate dose of Psilocybin. And now what you see is not just a hillside covered with Aspen trees in their full Fall colors, but Aspen trees that are dancing and interweaving with one another in a very sinuous and coordinated fashion, even moving across the far hillside. (Exper. #2)

In both cases, the immediate *feeling* you experience is one of awe and pleasure. It's a pleasant *feeling* experience. No interpretation yet required, that's just the way it feels to you at that point in time. But very quickly, almost simultaneously, you make a judgment about (you interpret) what is causing that feeling. In Exper. #1, you judge it to be the trees on the opposite hillside in their full Fall colors. In Exper. #2, you judge it to be the dancing and inter-movement among the trees as well as their colors which is making you feel so good and even, in awe.

In that immediate *feeling*, that awareness of how you feel at that moment, it seems you can't be wrong. You're simply reporting how you *feel* at that moment: warm/cold, pleasant/unpleasant, wanting more/wanting less. But in the second case, where you make a judgment about what is causing you to feel that way, you could be wrong. There may not be any trees on the far hillside, it may all be a very skillful and elaborate computer graphic display set up precisely to fool the casual passer-by. And similarly so for the person under the influence of psilocybin. What is causing their feeling of pleasure and awe, the trees dancing and swaying in a coordinated fashion, may, in fact, not be occurring at all. In both cases, the subsequent judgment (subsequent to the simple awareness of how you are feeling at that moment) introduces the possibility of error. In other words, there is the possibility of any such interpretation failing to be accurate. Failing to accurately capture exactly what was experienced, both in terms of what it was and what it reveals about reality, about the way 'things' really are.

2. Additional reasons for thinking the interpretation and the experience are distinct.

Here's another argument for this view, for the view that every experience involves an interpretation and that, in turn, introduces the possibility of error. If there were no gap between having an experience and *knowing* that it is an experience of _____, then

a.) anyone who has the experience could not be wrong about what it was an experience of. And

b) anyone who has the experience would come away from the experience in agreement with anyone else who had *the same* experience, as to what it was an experience of.

But, from the mundane to the exotic, has this, a.) & b.), ever been so? If not, it lends further weight to the view that any statement about an experience (beyond the purely phenomenological statement about how the experience is making you feel at the moment) involves an interpretation.

Einstein captured this reality beautifully in his remark to Werner Heisenberg:
> "Remember Werner, what we see is determined by the theory we use to interpret our observations."
>> (Where "observations" = the purely phenomenological description of what is striking one's eye and "see" = what we interpret those phenomena to be and how they were caused.)

[Another version of this same point:
> "I wouldn't have believed it if I hadn't seen it" is often true on one level, but
> "I wouldn't have seen it if I hadn't believed it" is always true at a deeper level.
>> "Believing Is Seeing . . ." by Michael Guillen]

Is Einstein right about this? It is the case, isn't it, that with any experience we have, we also (and virtually simultaneously) **interpret** that experience? I.e., we make a judgment about

(1) what the experience is "of", or *what* it is we are experiencing. And usually, closely attached in time to that interpretation, is another
(2) about <u>what is causing that experience</u>. And usually, our first such judgment about (2) is that <u>it is some feature of the world independent of us or of our minds which is causing that experience</u>. I.e., it is <u>not</u> something made up out of whole cloth by our own imagination.

3. Other conclusions that can be drawn from the fact that: all experience involves an interpretation.

There are two remaining points that I want to make. **The first** has to do with what, if anything, we might conclude from this observation and commentary by Einstein. And certainly one thing that seems obvious is that the experienc**er** is not the same thing as the experienc**ed**. What is experienced is what is being interpreted. That interpretation is being produced by the experiencer. Well, duhh! That seems pretty obvious. Ahhhhh, but note that if that's the case, if the experienc**er** and the experienc**ed** are two different things, then reality is dualistic (as opposed to monistic). There are subjects (the experienc**ers**) and objects (what is experienc**ed**). We will have more to say about this in Ch. 5, below.

The **second** point I want to make, given the Einstein quote above, is that the experienc**er** just is the same thing as "the self." Who or what is our "self"? It is that within us which experiences things. Therefore it is conscious (or is it consciousness itself?). And since, at our level (cf. the Great Chain of Being, Ch. 3), we are aware of our having these experiences, we are also self-conscious. And again, you might say, 'well, duh!' Of course there is an experienc**er** and an interpret**er**, a theory maker and a theory adopt**er**. But not everyone agrees! There are some worldviews (Buddhism, e.g.) which hold that there is "no-self". (But note that this very counter-intuitive view *may* be able to be made sense of and even defended, by resorting to what the Buddhist's refer to as "the Two Truths Doctrine." (Cf. Ch. 7 below & Chapter 11 of Bk. 3)

4. Does this possibility of error mean that experience can no longer be taken as evidence for the claim that something spiritual, some spiritual realm or reality, exists?

And now, back to our original question. In Ch. 3 (above), we considered experience as a possible source of **evidence for** the claim that something spiritual, some spiritual realm or reality, exists. Does what we are saying here undermine that claim? I.e., if all experience involves interpretation and as soon as interpretation is introduced, so also is the possibility of error, does that mean that experience cannot stand as evidence for the existence of something spiritual?

No. No more than the possibility of error in interpreting the results of scientific experiments invalidates those experiences as evidence for a particular conclusion. What it does mean is that we must be careful in coming to the conclusions/interpretations which we do come to. Making sure, e.g., that we don't let our desires for a particular outcome exceed the actual evidence. And some of the major ways we have of ensuring this, is repetition and peer review.

If every time we conduct a particular experiment, the (phenomenological) results are the same, and the theory we're using to interpret those observations is well-grounded and not to-date *dis*proven, then we are in a good position to trust our interpretation. And then, if others with the appropriate skills and background repeat the experiments and have the same results, and come to the same interpretations, then we have even greater confidence that we are at least justified in coming to the interpretation we have come to. This latter step is, in scientific circles, usually referred to as "peer review".

Well, the same can be depended upon in the spiritual realm. We can refer to those people who, by training, life style ("by their deeds shall you know them"), opportunity and experience are in a position to both have a "spiritual" experience and to interpret it correctly. So, a kind of "peer review" here as well? It seems so. (This approach is actually built into many of the Eastern religious traditions. There, it is often considered imperative that an aspirant find a guru or a teacher who has the requisite training and experience to both guide them along the path of discovery and to help them interpret whatever experiences they have along that path.) Thus, experience remains a viable source of evidence for the claim that there is a spiritual realm or reality. Albeit, one that is, for most of us, less easily accessed than is an experience of the results of a science experiment. (Though to be able to correctly interpret the results of many scientific experiments also requires a similarly rigorous training and background.)

And note that this process (peer review), which is the best we have so far, <u>does not guarantee</u> that the conclusion we come to is correct, it just gives us a reasonable basis for the conclusions we come to. This is so in science and it is also so in the other areas of our lives.

So the point(s) we're trying to make in Ch. 4 are?

Starting from experience as a way of establishing that something spiritual exists. [Ch. 3]

But identifying the cause and the meaning of any experience involves interpretation.

And as soon as interpretation is involved, so also is the possibility of error, error in identifying what exactly is being experienced as well as what is causing it.

But that need not rule out experience as a means of establishing the existence of something spiritual, for all those same problems are also true of any and all scientific experiments and we don't, on that account, reject scientific experiments as a means of establishing scientific truths.

Rather, we rely on peer review. And we can do the same in this area.

Chapter Outline   **Chapter 5**

Naive Realism, . . . Moderate Realism. . . or Idealism

Why important? What actually 'exists' and *how*? → What to believe . . . . and how to live.

1. **Simple/Naive Realism: Things are and are exactly as we see or experience them to be. Arguments against: 'Things' are not simply what they seem to be. E.g. color.**
   (Additional argument against: **the self**. It's not what/as it might initially seem?)

2. **Moderate Realism: Things are not (necessarily?) as we see or experience them to be, but they do exist, they do so independently of us and we can come to know *something* about how they are/exist independently of our perceiving apparatus. Ex's . . .**
   Arguments /evidence *for* moderate realism:
   Granted, many things are not as we experience them to be (contrary to naive realism), e.g. **color**. But we can come to know in part what they are and how they exist. E.g., via science. Consider also, **the self** and its implications for a moderate realism.

3. We can't *know* that anything other than our percepts and ideas actually exists.
   Kant's version of: . . .
     But, Kant's inconsistency: . . . .
   Buddhist: "And on another level, it's all just a dance of insubstantial appearances, . . ."
     But, what exactly is being said here? . . . .
       In one case the implication is that it's all like a desert mirage, whereas in
       the second case, the implication is that there is nothing "out there" at all!
         It all comes from and depends on the mind (or Mind?).
       Can something like a **"Two Truths Doctrine"** save the day? . . . .   (See also Ch. 6)

4. These ways of looking at and understanding what exists (moderate realism or idealism) lead to a couple of other key metaphysical concepts: **Dualism** and **Monism**.
   Why these are important.   Brief arguments pro and con.

5. **Conclusion**

Chapter 5
Moderate Realism vs. Idealism

In this chapter I want to consider three different ways of thinking about and understanding the world we live in. Three different ways in which we might think that 'things' exist. (I just used scare quotes around "things" in order to indicate that I don't want to impose any assumptions on exactly what is going to count as a thing. Basically, I will be using the term *thing* to mean or refer to anything that we might be able to come to know or be acquainted with. Henceforth, I'll omit the scare quotes.)

And why would this be important? Because how we answer this question: "what actually exists and *how* does it exist?" will, in large part, determine what we will believe and how we live, indeed, even how we think we *should* live.

Initially, it seems pretty obvious to most of us exactly *how* things exist. Whether we're talking about trees and cars or other people, planets, stars, and galaxies and even ideas, theories and mathematical formulas, we think of them as existing outside of us, or at least not dependent upon any one of us for their existence. These things are able to be known or acquainted with by other people and, in most instances, able to exist without any person around at all. (This last claim is problematic when it comes to ideas, thoughts, mathematical formulas, etc.. In mathematics, it's related to the problem of whether mathematical formulas, e.g., are invented or discovered. Does the notion, the idea, of political liberty exist independently of any person thinking it? Legitimate questions, but ones I'll pass on for now. And we'll focus, instead, on those things that are usually taken as existing or capable of existing, independently of any human mind thinking them or about them.)

This way of viewing things is generally referred to as **realism**. (Most) things are *real*. They exist outside of and independently of us. They can have an impact on us and we can come to know something(s) about them including that they do indeed exist independently of us. This broad category of realism may itself then be divided into two versions, one is usually referred to as *naive* realism and the other is called *moderate* realism.

1) Naive realism is the view that things outside of us exist *exactly* as we (through our senses) perceive them to exist. Thus, roses really are red (there is something called color that is in a rose, is red and is perceived by us as red); walls are solid (there is no space in a wall); that particular odor is in the thing I'm smelling, etc., etc.. But science has shown us that this way of thinking about what we perceive is wrong. The color of red is really the result of the way light bounces off that flower and is then filtered and interpreted by the rods and cones in our eyes. Similarly, the wall is only "solid" to something larger than the atoms that make up the wall (one's hand, e.g.). So virtually anyone who is acquainted with modern science has moved on from simple or naive realism to a moderate realism.

2) In a **moderate realism**, things still exist outside of and independently of us but not in a way that is *exactly* the way our senses present them to us. Our senses add and subtract aspects of the things we are acquainted with or come to know. Our senses act as filters or lenses, letting through some, but not all, of what exists "out there," independently of us. And beyond our senses, the concepts we use to understand and interrelate what we know are also partial and limited, focusing on some but not all of what any particular thing is. So, this view of things is *a realism*, things really do exist independently of us, but it is moderate in its recognition that the ways we experience things do not reveal them to us *exactly* as they are *in themselves* so to speak. Nevertheless, we can and do come to know them sufficiently accurately so that we can live with them, use them, predict how they will behave and, if we're talking about other people, come to know, care for and even love them.

Why might one think that moderate realism comes close to capturing the way things really are? Well, the first reason is that approaching things in this way seems the most functional and has proven to be very successful in terms of survival, prediction, manipulation, planning and execution. When we consider things in this way we're able to send men to the moon and to fix broken bones, cure or treat diseases, drive cars and prepare dinner, paint pictures, sculpt statues, compose and play music. This way of viewing things just **works very well**. And it also provides us with scientific explanations of what things are and how they work which, when tested, prove to be accurate.

Another reason for thinking that moderate realism comes close to capturing the way things really are, has to do with what we usually refer to as our **selves**. Each of us thinks that we have the ability and power to do things, to desire, to plan and execute strategies, to accomplish goals, to think and reason, to relate to other people, to feel happy and sad, remorseful and hopeful. We experience ourselves as having these powers and as being separate and independent from other people who have similar powers. Each of us seems to have their own particular way of viewing and interacting in the world and this helps distinguish me from you and all others. So, my self is different from your self and our selves are independent of one another (yours might exist without mine existing). All of which supports and exemplifies a moderate realism.

3) Well then, does everyone agree that moderate realism is the correct way to understand and think about how things exist in the world? No. They do not. There is another way of viewing how things exist in the world. It's called **idealism**. (And please note that in this context, the term *idealism*, does not refer to someone holding or professing some ideals as a preferred or especially admirable way of living. It's use here is more technical. It is referring to ideas and the way ideas exist.)

There are various versions of this way of viewing things. One of them comes from Immanuel Kant and is known as *transcendental idealism.* **Kant's view of things** is subtle and complex so my very short presentation of it here is going to be a simplification, but hopefully one that is accurate as far as it goes. Kant doesn't start with how things exist in the world, rather he starts with how we come to know about things that exist in the world. And he says that whatever we know about the world and things in the world, we know in terms of what we are given by our senses and our concepts. (And here is the pivotal point in his analysis.) So that what we know about the world and things in the world is actually what we are given by our senses and our concepts. And in that case, what we know are not the things in the world *as they actually are in themselves*, but as they are given to us through our sensations and concepts of them. Thus the idea-lism part. And further, we can never come to know how they actually are in themselves. What we know are 'ideas' (sensory and mind products), and, technically, that's all we can ever *know*.

Another form of idealism is that which is presented **in Buddhism** <u>at the level of</u> the Buddhist theorist or 'theologian'. At the level of the man-on-the-street, and even that of most simple monks, Buddhists live in and understand the world in a moderate realism sort of way. But when Buddhist scholars and theorists get to explaining things, they will often speak in terms of "everything comes from and is dependent upon the mind". Where "mind" sometimes seems to refer to any of our individual minds and at other times, to something like pure consciousness which individual minds tap into or are a part of. In either case, and at this level of understanding, we are dealing with an idealism. Ultimately, what's *real* is/are ideas (the 'products' of, in this case, pure consciousness).

But there are **problems with both** of these kinds of idealism. In Kant's case, he wants to be able to say that we <u>can</u> come to know the truth about the world, about how it really works, for example. And enough about our self to know that our cognitive faculties are reliable. But how could this be so if, as he asserts elsewhere, all we can know are <u>our representations of</u> what is given us by the world? He himself sees the problem and tries to solve it by appealing to a God who would not deceive us.

> "We must therefore think [of] an immaterial being, a world of understanding, and a Supreme Being . . . because in them only, as things in themselves, reason finds that completion and satisfaction, which it can never hope for in the derivation from appearance."
> Kant, Immanuel. *Prolegomena to Any Future Metaphysics*, 2nd. ed.
> Trans. James W. Ellington. Indianapolis, IN: Hackett, 2001. §57 B354-55*

But to appeal to such a reality "as things in themselves" essentially undermines his whole theory of transcendental idealism. If our minds are unreliable in getting us to what is true, to what is so, then they are unreliable also in claiming that we can't get to what is true and what is so.[*]

In Buddhism's case, the problem is different. Consider this statement from a long term Buddhist practitioner and teacher.

> "The great discovery in our practice is that, on one level, birth and death, existence and nonexistence, self and other are the great defining themes of our lives. And on another level, *it's all just a dance of insubstantial appearances*, what the Buddha called "the magic show of consciousness." [Emph. mine]
>
> Joseph Goldstein

This seems to be saying that really and ultimately, there are no 'things' at all, no substantial entities of any sort. There are only "insubstantial appearances." That would certainly fall into the category of an idealism. But then what kind of reality do "birth and death, existence and nonexistence, self and other" have? Are they all purely illusory?

And here, most Buddhist theorists turn to what they call the **Two Truths Doctrine** to navigate this dilemma. . . . Can something like the Two Truths Doctrine save the day?

What does **the Two Truths Doctrine** say or claim? Basically, that there are two levels, if you will, of existence. On one level, the

---

[*] I owe this insight to Peter Zuk's article: *Plantinga, Kant, and Cognitive Reliability*," in Global Tides Vol. 5, Article 2

level on which we live and move and have most of our being, there do indeed appear to be trees and cars, stars and other people all of which are not us, exist outside of and independently of us (they would go on existing even if we were to die and often existed even before we were born), and because of those features, seem to have some lasting substance. On that level, a moderate realism reigns.

But there is another level, a level on which 'things' have no substance at all ('no self' in Buddhist terminology), but are simply images or appearances conjured by our minds (or by Mind?). And on that level, what exists are only 'ideas' ("*insubstantial appearances*"). Thus, an idealism. And this level, according to these Buddhists, shows us the way 'things' *really* are. (This notion will come up again in a short while when it results in **dualism** on one level and **monism** on another.)

In Buddhism itself, e.g., on one level there are selves and the 8-fold path which one's self may or may not choose to follow; there is suffering and nirvana, all of which happen to a self. But ultimately, their scholars claim, it's all just **Buddha-nature**, and we, it, everything, already is that.

But there are **problems with the Two Truths Doctrine**. For it's claiming that differences, e.g., between you and Josef Stalin or between you and the tree in the front yard, or between you and Mt. Everest, **are secondary** and **ultimately illusory**. Really and ultimately, (at their core), all of these are the same in that they are all just manifestations of one thing, call it consciousness or Consciousness.

But then, wouldn't it be the case that *ultimately* it doesn't make any difference how you live your life, since ultimately the outcome, the final state, must be the same? Indeed, the final state is not different from the present state except, perhaps, in one's awareness of it. In Buddhism, e.g., they say we already have/are **Buddha Nature**. In that regard, we are already in our final state, we just don't realize it. And note how this would affect your conception of your self. Indeed, and not just your conception of your self, but any actual self there might be. . . . .

4) And thus we go from *what we know and can know* about the world and the things that are in it, to *what actually exists* (from a naive realism to a moderate realism to an idealism). And this, in turn, leads us to the question of whether, ultimately, only **one** *kind* of thing exists, ideas e.g. or consciousness or Buddha Nature (= a **monism**), or, again ultimately, **more than one** *kind* of thing exists, e.g. the physical or material and the spiritual; the composed and the not- composed; matter-energy and intelligence (consciousness?) And this would be a **dualism**.

Who worries about stuff like this? And why would one??! It seems arcane, abstract, technical and of no practical consequence what-so-ever. But, it turns out, how you answer it determines many other things. For example, if you adopt **a monistic worldview**, then either God (as the Western monotheisms conceive of Him/Her/It) would not exist or material things would not exist (because the creator-creature dichotomy would not exist).

In this monistic worldview you and God would, ultimately, just be the same thing. Here's a fun little example of this latter.

I have a good friend who converted to Hinduism. He was raised in a Catholic family and in the Catholic tradition. In fact, he even entered a Jesuit monastery to train for the priesthood before deciding that wasn't for him. When I asked him recently what he thought of, and how he came to accept, **the monism** of Hinduism*, he gave me a one word response. *Namasté*. His thought was that that one word and the concepts behind it sufficed to explain both what he thought was true and, presumably, *why* he thought it was true.

That same friend then recounted a marvelous little experience he had in India not too long ago which also illustrates the monism we have been speaking of and how it might affect someone's life. I'll let his own words convey this story.

> "Once, on the ghats along Ganga Mata (the Ganges, in India: "mother Ganga"), I met someone who asked me if I knew god. "Yes," I said. And he replied, "So, who is god? Where is god?" I replied, "You are. You are here." The Sadhu, with whom I was speaking, then said, "Yes". And went on his way."
>
>> [A Sadhu in India is a religious, itinerant mendicant. Someone who has rejected the things of this world in order to dedicate themselves to prayer, fasting and self-abnegation in pursuit of *moksha* (liberation from the cycle of birth, death and rebirth). Sometimes also referred to as a "forest dweller".]

So, ultimately which is it? **Monism** or **dualism**? Self or no-self, subjects and objects or neither? Or can both be true albeit on different levels? (The Two Truths Doctrine, e.g..)

* What I'm referring to in the text above as the "monism" of Hinduism requires some explanation. Most people who may be at least passingly familiar with Hinduism would be surprised, if not shocked, at hearing that Hinduism is a monism. Doesn't it have multiple deities and avatars many of whom are separately worshiped by Hindus? Yes, it certainly does. But a full history and explanation here of why it might nevertheless be said to be a monism would take us way too far afield. So I'll let the following suffice for our purposes here to explain *how* Hinduism might still be thought of as a monism. In the briefest possible explanation: Brahman is thought of as the supreme deity in Hinduism and all the other gods and goddesses are either dependent upon him or partial expressions of his nature (the avatars, e.g.). Similarly so with everything else that exists. It all comes from and depends upon Brahman and **in that sense** there is just one 'thing', reality is monistic. And it was in that sense that my friend was using the term *Namasté*. An English translation of *that sense* might go: All is one and all is God.]

And note that the Western monotheisms face a somewhat similar dilemma, viz. how can there be anything not-God, anything outside of God, so-to-speak? Wouldn't that limit God? But if all is within God, then isn't everything God? The solution to this dilemma which is most often adopted, seems to hinge on the notion of *dependence*. If something is dependent upon God for its existence, then it is not separate from God, and in that sense, not outside of God, but it is not God.

****

Finally, if one is looking for **an *argument* against monism** here is one of the better ones I have yet to see.

"What is more, as Daniel Robinson argues, **neuroscience in particular has implicitly dualist commitments**, because the correlation of brain states with mental states would be a waste of time if we did not have independent evidence that these mental states existed. It would make no sense, for example, to investigate the neural correlates of pain if we did not have independent evidence of the existence of pain from the subjective experience of what it is like to be in pain. This evidence, though, is not scientific evidence: it depends on introspection (the self becomes aware of its own thoughts and experiences), which again assumes the existence of mental subjects. Further, Richard Swinburne has argued, scientific attempts to show that mental states are epiphenomenal* are self-refuting, since they require that mental states reliably cause our reports of being in those states. The idea, therefore, that science has somehow shown the irrelevance of the mind to explaining behavior is seriously confused." [emph. mine]

> *Minding the Brain: Models of the Mind, Information, and Empirical Science*, Edited by Angus J. L. Menuge, Brian R. Krouse, and Robert J. Marks.

*[Epiphenomenalism is the view that mental events are caused by physical events in the brain, but have no effects upon any physical events.]

5) In conclusion, what exists? What is real? *How* does the world (the cosmos, the universe, everything that exists), *how* does it exist? Does a **moderate realism** capture the reality, or is it rather an **idealism**?

And does **a dualism** most accurately reflect the way 'things' really are or is it all, ultimately, just one, **a monism**? And how would each of these affect how you might live your life, what you might believe in, what you might strive for? Indeed, which of these worldviews is actually reflected in the way you <u>do</u> live your life, what you <u>do</u> believe in and what you <u>do</u> strive for?

Chapter Outline   **Chapter 6**

An Important Distinction and Its Impact

1. Connection to previous Chapter & **monism** or **dualism**.

2. **Idealistic monism**.
   What it is and its seeming absurdity.
   > Common arguments *against* monism, from Samuel Johnson's to our normal daily living.

3. But, there are some reasons to take it seriously.
   Many smart people over the ages have held it to be so.
   An argument from *how* we know to *what* we know.
   > (But doesn't this leave us with a knower and the known, i.e. a dualism?)

4. And there is a possible 'escape hatch' for explaining away our common, everyday experience, viz. the **Two Truths Doctrine**.
   And so, there remain at least two reasons *for* considering idealistic monism.

5. BUT, there's **a critical distinction** embedded in any idealistic monism.
   Any ultimate reality, whether Consciousness or Mind or the "ultimate implicate order" is conceived of as the source for everything else.
   And this source **is not dependent** while all that comes from the source **is dependent**, namely, it's dependent upon that source for its existence.
   Buddha himself recognized and spoke of this distinction. – *Udana* 8.3
   But then, we have two things that are not the same. Nothing designated as **dependent** can be the same as something designated as **not dependent**.
   (See commentary on **Leibniz's law** in Chapter 7.)
   But this distinction, then, entails a dualism, and in this way, idealistic monism, as usually conceived, is shown to be self-refuting. And the Two Truths Doctrine cannot save the day.

Chapter 6
An Important Distinction and Its Impact

1) The connection between this chapter and the previous chapter comes from what was talked about toward the end of that previous chapter, viz. dualism and monism. To briefly re-cap: **dualism** is the view that there are, basically, two different kinds of things that make up everything that exists and that these two cannot be reduced to just one of them. Typically, the two 'things' thought of when considering dualism are matter and spirit, or mind and body. **Monism** is the view that, ultimately, there is just one 'thing' that makes up everything that exists. What that one thing is varies from monism to monism, but the two leading candidates are: matter (or the matter-energy dyad) and 'ideas' or the products of mind or consciousness, or simply consciousness itself. The latter form of monism is also referred to as **idealistic monism** or simply **idealism**.

2) But given what we saw in the previous chapter about idealism, even the curious reader might wonder *why* we're bothering about this at all. On the surface, it seems to be a fairly easily dismissed view of things. Consider, e.g., Dr. Johnson's brusque "I refute him (Berkeley and his idealism) thus" by simply kicking a stone in his path. And it's not at all clear that such a view of things has any meaningful impact at all on our daily living. In fact, it seems pretty clear, in that daily living, that I am not you and you are not me; that an idea is not a truck, that God, if any such exists, is not a giraffe and that anything spiritual is, virtually by definition, nothing material. So why concern ourselves with this?

3) There are at least two reasons. **The first** is, as was mentioned above, that there have been serious thinkers in the past and today who believe that some form of monism <u>is</u> true. Each of these ways of trying to understand the world has had its adherents and proponents over the centuries. Monism, from Heraclitus and Parmenides among the ancient Greeks to the later, and usually idealistic monism, of Bishop Berkeley and Hegel in the 17th and 18th centuries, to many modern Buddhists in today's world. And dualism, from Plato and Aristotle to Descartes and Kant and most of the rest of us. And that, naturally enough, leads to a question about *why* would such smart people believe such a thing.

And **second**, there is this argument which has been used in the past to get to idealism goes something like this:

> What we know is given to us through our senses.
> And this "given" is then construed, constructed and interrelated by means of our concepts.
> So what we really end up knowing is our ideas or concepts.
> So why think there are 'things' *out there* at all? All we know that exists are our ideas.
> Hence, idealism is so.

4) In addition, it turns out that the proponents of such a view argue something like this: "yes, yes, in our normal daily living we live *as though* dualism is the case" *I* am <u>not</u> you, that truck racing down the street will squash me if I step out in front of it, and a thought, an idea, an imagined entity is not the same thing or even the same kind of thing as this chair I'm sitting on. And the language we speak enshrines this view of things: that there are subjects and objects and they are not all the same thing nor the same kind of 'thing'. But then the monist will add something like this: 'but, that is only at the level on which we live our daily lives. There is another, more basic level, a level on which we come to understand that everything that is (any and everything that exists) is really just an expression of, is totally reliant upon, one kind of thing. Matter-energy for the materialistic monist or Mind / Consciousness, for the idealistic monist. Buddhism explicitly refers to this way of viewing things as the **Two Truths Doctrine**.

According to this latter way of looking at things, the way things are (or appear to be) on the level on which we live our daily lives, is true, . . . *as far as it goes*. It's just that it is incomplete, it is not revealing to us the whole story, if you will. There is another level which does that. And on that level, there is just one 'thing'. Within Buddhism, it is often called Buddha Nature as was mentioned before.

And here's a Buddhist scholar trying to give a more precise description / definition of what that one, primordial, thing is.

> "According to this view [the Great Perfection system and theory of Dzogchen within Buddhism], the physical world, the form realm and the formless realm all emerge from an implicate unity of the absolute space of phenomena (*dharmadhātu*), primordial consciousness (*jñāna*), and a primal energy (*jñāna-prāna*) that is indivisible from both space and consciousness. The absolute space of phenomena is not to be confused with relative space; rather, it is the ultimate dimension of reality out of which space, time, energy, matter, and mind all emerge. This

primordial unity of space, consciousness, and energy is the ultimate implicate order."

B. Alan Wallace,

<u>Hidden Dimensions</u>, *The Unification of Physics and Consciousness*, p. 110.
2007 Columbia University Press, N.Y.

(Whew! Hmmm?)

5) Sooooo, which is it? Dualism or monism? Or both, via something like the Two Truths Doctrine? I think *it looks like* both. But the distinction most often used to make this solution work, <u>if properly understood</u>, actually leads back to a fundamental dualism. I like to think of this as, (if you'll allow me to borrow a somewhat modified line from a Paul Newman movie (Cool Hand Luke):

"What we have here is a failure to ~~communicate~~ distinguish."

And that distinction is between the **dependent** and the **not-dependent** or between the contingent and the necessary. Let me explain.

The distinction I am referring to is when they say that everything we encounter in our daily living is, ultimately, <u>dependent upon</u> some one thing. In Wallace's words (above) that one thing is an "implicate unity" (here he is expanding on a concept from David Bohm–viz. that of "the implicate order"). That is, the one thing from which everything else comes and on which everything else depends. And *in that sense*, it's all– everything that exists is– just one.

But the fact that x <u>depends on</u> y for what it is and for its existence does not mean or entail that x = y. A painting or a piece of sculpture, a poem or a symphony all depend for their existence on the artist or author or composer who created them. But none of them are equal to or are the same as their artist or author or composer.

Similarly so for everything that exists in the phenomenal realm (the realm of what we experience through our senses) and beyond that to anything and everything that depends on another for its existence. What exists <u>dependently</u>, is not the same thing as whatever might exist <u>non-dependently</u>.

The Buddha himself recognized this distinction at *Udana* 8.3, when he says:

> "There is, bhikkhus, **a not-born, a not-brought-to-being, a not-made, a not-conditioned**. If, bhikkhus, there were no not-born, not-brought-to-being, not-made, not-conditioned, no escape would be discerned from **what is born, brought-to-being, made, conditioned**. But since there is a not-born, a not-brought-to-being, a not-made, a not-conditioned, therefore an escape is discerned from what is born, brought-to-being, made, conditioned."
>
> [emph. mine]
> – The Buddha, speaking to a gathering of monks and nuns sometime in the 5th century, B.C.E. From the Pali Canon, *Udana* 8.3
> Translated from the Pali by John D. Ireland

A "not-conditioned" and a "conditioned". But if this is the case, we are beyond monism. For he is asserting that <u>there is</u> a "not-born, not-brought-to-being, not-made, not-conditioned" as well as a "born, brought-to-being, made, (and) conditioned." Pretty clearly, two different *kinds* of things.

(Traditionally, this same distinction has been recognized by all of the Abrahamic religions and enshrined in their concepts of creature and creator. Two different kinds of things, which are not the same.)

But is that going from what *could* be the case (the existence of a creator or of a not-conditioned) to what actually *is* the case? Good question, but it will have to be left for another 'day'. Here, I am only concerned with pointing out that if the monists believe, and they certainly seem to, that there is an ultimate source of everything, for whatever exists in whatever manner, then that universe *must be* construed as a dualism. A dualism of the dependent and the not-dependent or of the contingent and the non-contingent, or as the Buddha has it, of the conditioned and the not-conditioned. Again, the fact that x wholly depends on y for its existence does not entail or mean that x = y.

And this is important because? Or, and this leaves us where? It leaves us with a more accurate understanding of what is the case, with denying any ultimate monism and rejecting the claim that anything like the Two Truths Doctrine will save the day for the monists.

And please note:

I am NOT arguing that because we can conceive of something that is non-dependent, or necessary, or not conditioned, such a thing actually exists. No. I do not think that we can go from simply being able to conceive of something to the claim that such actually exists (with all deference to Anselm). Rather, and what I *am* arguing is that IF one claims that there is a not-conditioned (as the Buddha does) or an "ultimate implicate order" (as Wallace does), then one is committed to a dualism, viz. the dualism of the not-conditioned and the conditioned, or of the "ultimate implicate order" and everything else which comes from but isn't that.

Chapter Outline   **Chapter 7**

Don't be so open-minded that your brains fall out.

1. **No-self**
   Buddhism claims there is "no-self" in anything, and therefore not in us. In short, we neither have nor are a self. But this conflicts not only with what we think (know?) to be true about ourselves and others, it conflicts with what Buddhism itself teaches and practices at the level of the common person. This *may* be resolvable by focusing on the different meaning they use for the term 'substance' but it seems to go further than that to a denial of any unitary source of our own activity. And that would seem to require them to claim that both our actions and what we experience are just unsourced happenings. (??)

2. **The Two Truths Doctrine**
   Reasons for thinking it may be true: who has proposed it and the problem it "solves".
   But, in solving that problem, it opens itself to an even more fundamental problem, viz. a commitment to **a** metaphysical **dualism**. (A "problem" only because Buddhism, ultimately, claims to be an idealistic **monism**.)
   And we encounter again the distinction between the **de**pendent and the **not-de**pendent. Which, as we saw in the last Chapter, entails a metaphysical dualism.
   But to assert a theory which purports to explain how reality is a monism, but which theory itself requires a fundamental dualism is incoherent. And to accept an incoherent theory is, in effect, to let "your brains fall out".

3. **Shutting down the discursive, analytic mind**
   Achieving enlightenment by way of contemplation or shutting down the discursive, analytic mind.
   Many traditions, both East and West make claims that this can be done.
   So, maybe knowledge can be achieved/acquired in this way.
   > Certainly, the monks and nuns, Roshis, gurus and saints who have claimed that this can be done constitute (by the lives they lead and the time spent practicing in this way) some grounds for thinking that indeed it can.

   But even if knowledge can be acquired in this way, it would **not be communicable** in language. To be communicable, one has to speak using words which involve concepts and ideas. And both of those, if they are going to be clear, accurate and intelligible, require thinking and analysis.

Chapter 7
Don't be so open-minded that your brains fall out.

This chapter considers three different concepts within Buddhism and finds each of them problematic. Nor are these concepts peculiar to or restricted to Buddhism, it's just that that's the form or understanding of them that we'll be focusing on in this chapter. The first of these is:

1) No-self

According to Buddhism, there is **no self**, in anything and therefore not 'in' us. Here, e.g., is one commentator's view of what the Dalai Lama would say:

In his foreword to "A Profound Mind: Cultivating Wisdom in Everyday Life" by His Holiness the Dalai Lama, Nicholas Vreeland wrote,

> "Perhaps the chief difference between Buddhism and the world's other major faith traditions lies in its presentation of our core identity. **The existence of the soul or self**, which is affirmed in different ways by Hinduism, Judaism, Christianity, and Islam, **is** not only **firmly denied in Buddhism**; belief in it is identified as the chief source of all our misery. The Buddhist path is fundamentally a process of learning to recognize this essential nonexistence of the self, while seeking to help other sentient beings to recognize it as well." [emph. mine]

(And given the source (in a book written by the Dalai Lama himself), I think we can assume that the Dalai Lama agrees with the author of the Forward in that same book.)

Initially, it seems, such a view of "no-self" cannot be thought or said coherently. '*I* don't have any I.'?? Or, 'There is no self, no subject, who is thinking these thoughts or asking these questions or being kind to my neighbor.' Huh?

We are accustomed to thinking of ourselves as beings who experience things, who think, desire, will, choose, enjoy and suffer among various other activities. So if someone says that really and ultimately there is no one "in there" that is doing all these things, it is at least puzzling if not incomprehensible. For if there is no one "in there", no subject, where are these thoughts, desires, choices, actions etc. coming from? According to this no-self view, from no individual and no where. (Or, perhaps, from mind? Or Mind??) They are just happening. And <u>to whom</u> are they happening? No one. They are happening <u>in</u> our body-brain and that body-brain interprets them as coming from us, from a self within us. Whoops! "interprets"? Couldn't have <u>that</u> without someone, a self?, a subject? a something which does the interpreting, no?

This puzzle is further emphasized because so much of Buddhist doctrine and practice seems to presume just the opposite, that we do have/just are such a self. From listening to (now reading) the Buddha's teachings or those of other Buddhist gurus and Roshis, to following instructions, to deciding to and actually undertaking meditation, to believing that the 8-fold path really is the way to achieve enlightenment, and to actually achieving such enlightenment. All of these seem to assume that <u>some</u> <u>one</u> is doing these things, some self is doing them. And that your self is not the same as my self. For example, you may choose to follow Buddhism and I may decide not to, so your self is not the same thing as my self. So what could it possibly mean to say that there is **no-self**, in anything, anywhere?

On its face, it seems absurd. And here is an example from a Western commentator which illustrates just one aspect of such absurdity since it would deny the continuity of our selves over time.

> "Furthermore, scientific inquiry assumes that it is one and the same conscious subject that has a research question, and persists over the time necessary to answer that question. How can a scientist claim to discover the answer to his question, or to verify or falsify a prediction that he made, if he is not the very same person that asked the question or made the prediction? For example, consider François Englert and Peter Higgs, who predicted the existence of the Boson nearly fifty years before its existence was confirmed. When these scientists became Nobel Prize winners in 2013, everyone assumed that the very same persons receiving the prize made the prediction decades before. Yet due to the constant flux of matter in our physical bodies and brains over time, physicalist approaches to personal identity find it very difficult to justify this assumption."
>
> *Minding the Brain: Models of the Mind, Information, and Empirical Science*, edited by Angus J. L. Menuge, Brian R. Krouse, and Robert J. Marks.

But *maybe* this seeming incoherence can be solved by pointing out a difference in the way certain terms are being used.

For the Buddhists who make this claim it seems to mean . . . . there is nothing *substantial* in us, where that term, *substantial*, is taken to mean: able to exist all on its own, independently of any and all other entities, in no way "dependently-arisen," or <u>not dependent</u> in *any* way.

But this is a very different meaning to 'substance' than what most Western philosophers and thinkers have meant by it since at least Plato and Aristotle. Here in the West, when people speak of something's substance they are usually referring to whatever it is that makes the thing in question to be the thing that it is. Usually, <u>the sort of thing</u> that it is but sometimes, also, the particular thing that it is within that category of things. Thus the substance of this apple is that it is a certain kind of tree fruit. And this particular apple is differentiated from all the rest of those same kinds of tree fruit because it has a certain degree of roundness or color or weight or blemishes or a particular combination of all of these characteristics. (These latter characteristics are usually thought of as being "secondary characteristics" of the apple because they don't change the fact that it's a particular kind of tree fruit.)

So then, can we solve the problem simply by saying that what most people mean by their "self" is nothing like what the Buddhists seem to be requiring of such?. Can we simply say: 'certainly we <u>are</u> all <u>inter</u>dependent, <u>but there is something there</u> which <u>does exist</u>. E.g., it may exist as one node in an interdependent web of nodes (Indra's Net). But that something is what we are referring to when we refer to our self. And that most certainly does exist. For something to exist *interdependently*, it must at least exist; "nothing" cannot be dependent on or interdependent with anything.

Indeed, can anything, according to the Buddhists, exist without being dependently arisen? It's not clear. The Buddha, at Udana 8.3 (above, p. 67) e.g., would seem to indicate that something <u>does</u>

<u>indeed</u> exist in that way. And Wallace's "implicate order" (above, p. 66) also seems to exist in that way. So it seems that at least some Buddhist scholars (not to mention the Buddha himself) think that there is something that can be called a substance in that quite specific Buddhist sense of the term.

So, is the solution to the apparent problem simply to say: when the Buddhists say there is "no-self" they are referring to something which no one is claiming <u>does exist in the way they're requiring</u>? (I.e., when we speak of our selves, we are <u>not</u> referring to something which can and does exist all by itself, without any dependence on or interdependence with other existent entities.)

Unfortunately, no. That will not solve the problem. For if there is no self which is doing the acting and experiencing what happens to it, where are those activities and experiences coming from according to the Buddhists? From nowhere and nothing? They are just uncaused happenings, period. But that so flies in the face of how we understand and interpret our own experience and the world, as to be virtually incomprehensible. If that were the case, there would be no way of explaining the continuity we all experience both in defining our selves, and in interpreting our experience. See quote above from *Minding the Brain*. The title of this chapter looms.

2) The Two Truths Doctrine

The Two Truths Doctrine is the claim that there is one way of describing things which is true *at the level of how we live our daily lives* and something quite different (even contradictory to it) which is true at the level of how things *really* are.

And it's easy to understand how this might be. Science itself tells us just this sort of thing when it speaks of atoms and electrons and quarks and, possibly, strings. There is a level on which 'things' are very, very different from what they appear to us to be on the level of our daily experience. But for the most part, scientists do not then go from that fact to a claim about monism. In their situation, it would be *a materialistic* monism. Some do, of course, but many remain agnostic on the subject or at least admit that it confronts them with a "hard problem", viz. the problem of how to explain consciousness as coming from anything material. (See Ch. 9 below.)

There is a further reason why we are or might be inclined to accept the Two Truths Doctrine and that is the background and character of the scholars and monks who have proposed it. By and large they are good people and people who have spent years and years studying, meditating and reflecting on the contents and activities of their minds. It's easy to conclude from this that they very likely have discovered something about how our minds work and their contents. And if those discoveries have led them to propose or accept the True Truths Doctrine, then that seems to be at least a reason for thinking it true.

But, more often, the main reason such monks and scholars move toward a Two Truths Doctrine is that it appears to solve a genuine problem. And that problem is that when we consider what we can and do *know*, we discover that all of our phenomenal experience is incomplete and structured in a very particular way by our senses. Which, naturally enough, leads to the question: well then, but what are things *really* like?

In addition, when approached from the standpoint of metaphysics, there seems to be a problem with everything being **de**pendent. If everything is **de**pendent (contingent), couldn't there be a time when nothing existed? And if you can't get something from nothing, how do we explain that something exists now?

The Two Truths Doctrine appears to solve both of these problems. Things as we experience them *are really* "just a dance of insubstantial appearances." And not everything is **de**pendent because "Buddha Nature" or "the absolute space of phenomena" is <u>not</u> dependent.

Unfortunately, in solving these two problems, the Two Truths Doctrine creates another one for its proponents and one which fundamentally conflicts with the metaphysics required by the Two Truths Doctrine itself.

As we saw in the last chapter, the Two Truths Doctrine ultimately claims to be a monism. It holds that really, only one thing truly exists. Everything else is fundamentally illusory, it appears as one kind of thing, something independent of us e.g., but is actually another, a product of mind or consciousness ("everything comes from and depends on the mind") and *in that way* it is all illusory.

We argued against this conclusion in the previous chapter based on the distinction between something being dependent and something else being not-dependent. I want to fill out that argument a little bit, here, and in doing so justify the somewhat smartalecky title of this chapter.

I showed in the last chapter that the Two Truths Doctrine ultimately proposes an idealistic monism. There is only one thing that truly exists and everything else is nothing more than an ephemeral, constantly changing, appearance. And the Buddhists have different names for that one thing. I then argued that that very way of viewing things actually required a dualism, not a monism, a dualism of the **de**pendent and the **not-de**pendent. And this argument is itself reliant upon a logical principle which I now want to spend just a little time explicating.

The principle in question is usually attributed to Wilhelm Gottfried Leibniz and is known as **Leibniz's Law** or, variously, as The Identity of Indiscernibles and alternatively as the Non-identity of Discernibles. It may be stated thusly:

> If any object, x, has all and only the same properties as object y, then x is identical to y. Alternatively: If x has a property that y does not have, then x and y are not the same.

Well, "duhhh" you might think. That seems pretty obvious, and you can't imagine how anyone could ever argue against it. (But some have. Those philosophers !!) Nevertheless, we are going to take it as true and incontrovertible as it seems to be. And even though it seems pretty simple and quite obviously true, it turns out that it can have great effect on how we understand things.

In the last chapter, I applied it to the distinction between the **de**pendent and the **not-de**pendent, arguing that if something were dependent then it could not be the same thing as something which was not-dependent. And based on that argument, I further argued that if a theory or worldview proposed or entailed this distinction, then that worldview *must be* a dualism. There was, in such a worldview, two different kinds of things, viz. the **de**pendent and the **not-de**pendent. And this would conflict with any monistic view of things. And on this basis, I further argued that something like a Two Truths Doctrine, though it might solve a problem on the surface, so to speak, created a more significant problem underneath. (A "problem" if the proponents of that particular worldview wanted to subscribe to a metaphysical monism.)

It is at this point, that I think the title of this chapter especially applies. For to assert a worldview of the sort we've been considering, a view in which there is some one thing which is **not-dependent** (not contingent, not conditioned) along with other things (whether ideas or trucks or mountains) which are **dependent** and to then further assert that this view constitutes a monism, is to fly in the face of Leibniz's Law. And doing that, I would contend, is equivalent to being so "open-minded that your brains fall out". One can hold a Two Truths Doctrine, but in doing so one is committed to a metaphysical dualism. A dualism of the **de**pendent and the **non-de**pendent.

The Two Truths Doctrine works when it's restricted to simply asserting that there are levels of truth, e.g. the phenomenal level and the fundamental science level. Perhaps even, the social-psychological level of having/being a self and the metaphysical level of no-self (depending on how 'self' is interpreted). But these are something we knew already and have known for some time. (Perhaps as far back as the 5th century BCE in both the East and the West when it comes to the phenomenal level of experience and the scientific attempt to explain what's behind/underneath that phenomenal level.) But it fails if and when it is used to establish any metaphysical monism. It cannot do away with, in fact it depends upon, the distinction between the

dependent and the **non-de**pendent. And those **two** are not and cannot be the same. Hence, no monism.

3) Shutting down the discursive, analytic mind.

In many of the religious traditions, both East and West, meditation/contemplation is thought to be an important tool (and sometimes, even, a necessary tool) for achieving enlightenment. Where enlightenment is taken to mean coming to 'see' the way 'things' *really* are. The way whatever is real exists and is structured. Not in any scientific way, but involving and focusing on the spiritual realm. And again, in both the East and the West, the highest form of such meditation is thought to be a form of meditation which transcends thinking about anything. In Buddhism (and Hinduism), e.g., the progress goes from *shamatha*, which involves learning how to achieve and maintain a one-pointed attention on a given object or image or idea, to *vipassana* which involves simply 'seeing' the mind, its relation to one's body and all that transpires within the mind. (Note that these descriptions of meditation, both East and West, are by no means, and are not meant to be, complete. Rather, they are meant to give the reader at least some understanding of what is being talked about and its place in these religious traditions.)

And in the West, there is also a similar progress from meditation (thinking about biblical passages, e.g. and what they mean and how they should affect one's life) to contemplation where the process is one of just 'looking' at some episode in Christ's life or one of his teachings. A relatively recent development in this latter area has become known as "centering prayer".

In both traditions, one ends up transcending any analytic, discursive thought process and reaches a state when one just 'sees' (knows) what is the case. And once that stage has been achieved, it is presumed, one's life orientation and behavior changes to reflect and express what one has come to know in this way. In both Buddhism and Hinduism, one has achieved enlightenment. In the Abrahamic religions, it is most often referred to as a mystical insight.

And again, in both traditions (East and West), many practitioners, many monks and nuns, hermits, sadhus, dervishes, followers of kabbalah, etc. have devoted their lives to achieving this level of meditation and, at least for some of them, claim to have succeeded in achieving enlightenment. (Though it is interesting to note how rare it is to hear of anyone of these practitioners actually claiming to have achieved enlightenment. I take this as more of a testimony to their humility and carefulness than to the fact that it's never been done.) And this history then, leads one to think that indeed it can be done. This is at least a, if not the way, of achieving enlightenment.

But here's the problem. Even if we assume that this is a way to achieve enlightenment (the only way?), the resultant 'knowledge' would not be able to be explained. Since it came to the practitioner not as a result of thinking and analyzing but simply as a (supposed) insight, they would not have any grounds for explaining how and why it is true. They would have the conviction that it is, but their conviction would be untethered to facts and reasons. And though it could still be true, there would be no way of explaining or showing *why* or *how* it is true. About all one could do would be to say: 'go through the same steps which I have gone through and you will very likely have the same experience I had and, as a result of that experience, you will come to *know* what I am now convinced of.'

Well,. . . . that would be so *only if* you **interpreted** the experience in the same way as the guru has (look back at Ch. 4 where we showed that all experience involves an interpretation). And the problem with that is, at least in the Eastern traditions, it's the guru him/herself who decides how you should interpret your experience. Woahhh. The chance of self-dealing in such a situation is significant. (Even if we assume honesty and well-meaning on the part of the guru, the inclination of their part to interpret your experience in accordance with whatever they have been teaching you would be great indeed.)

The up-shot is, if we shut down the discursive and analytic mind we will not be able to communicate whatever it is we think we have come to know since any such communication necessarily involves using concepts and ideas and the various relationships that can exist among them. And that just is analysis. No analysis, no communicable knowledge. Maybe you can have knowledge by way of insight, but to be communicated you have to use the discursive, analytic tools we use in all other cases of communicating knowledge.

So, accepting the following sort of claim: "I 'saw' that this is the way things are and even though I can't explain how they could be that way or why, you should accept what I'm saying as true." Would again seem to elicit the warning that heads this chapter.

Chapter Outline   **Chapter 8**

Why Did The Universe Begin?
(But the real subject is the principle of sufficient reason.)

1. **Introduction (But not central to the thesis. Just sets up the relationship between the principle of sufficient reason and the title of this chapter.)**
   Similarity of two questions: . . . . .
   But they are different. One presumes the universe did begin, the other does not.
   > We'll be focusing on the one that presumes it did have a beginning.
   > (Though what we say will also apply equally to the case where it did not.)

2. **And it will turn out that this question itself leads to something even more basic. Viz. the principle of sufficient reason.**
   This principle states that . . .
   This is ambiguous, but in a very rich way.
   > It could be talking metaphysically, i.e. . . . . .
   > Or it could be a definition of rationality and understanding.
   > I'm going to focus on this latter.

3. **The principle of sufficient reason now applied to our original question.**
   Oooops! No reason why, it just did. A purely random, surd event.
   Creation
   Other possibilities?

4. **And here are some notable quotes which reflect just this sort of understanding.**

Chapter 8
Why Did The Universe Begin? (cf. also Bk.1, Ch. 5)

1) Introduction This question is very similar to the question: why is there something at all? Or, why is there something rather than nothing? Which itself has been called **"the fundamental question of metaphysics"**. Which makes it fit right into the subjects we're examining in this little book.

But there is also a difference between these two questions and that difference will itself make a difference in how we proceed to examine the question heading this chapter. And the difference is that the question which heads this chapter assumes that the universe *did begin* at some time. Or, alternatively, that there was a time when the universe did not exist. This (that the universe did begin at some time) is a huge assumption that not everyone agrees with. Whereas the other question presumes only that something does actually exist now. (Note that by "universe" I am referring to all the matter and energy that exists anywhere and everywhere. This concept is also sometimes referred to as *the cosmos*.)

The alternative view (to the universe beginning at some time) is that the universe, in some form, has always existed. Probably the most common way of conceiving of this alternative is to think of the universe as cyclical. For example, from a very small and simple beginning it grows in both complexity and size until it collapses back on itself. And then the cycle repeats. As I understand their cosmology, this, e.g., is what Hinduism (and Buddhism) believe, as well as what some modern astrophysicists hold: there has never been a time when the universe did not exist at some level of size and complexity. Within Hinduism, these periods of time during which a particular universe exists are known, as *Kalpas* and their pictorial descriptions are marvelously inventive and fun to picture. Here, e.g., is one such.

> Imagine a bird with a silk scarf held in its beak and as it flies over Mt. Everest, it lets that scarf rub against the top of the mountain. In the time it would take for that action to rub Mt. Everest down to ground level, just 1 year of a Kalpa's existence would have passed.

At first glance, such a cyclical universe appears to contradict the current Big Bang theory about the start of our universe, but it needn't be seen that way. The Big Bang could simply have been the start of our *current* universe after the collapse of some former universe. So such a view does not contradict the current widely held astrophysical view of the start of our universe.

Note also that the cyclical answer amounts to saying that something physical, some form of matter-energy, has always existed. For if it has not always existed and yet something exists now, then there was a time when things had to begin from nothing. Note further that I think one can assert that "has always existed" position without asserting or depending on any claim that matter-energy itself *must* exist or cannot not exist or exists necessarily. (Though it does seem a stretch to say that something which can go out of existence has not, in fact, *ever*, in infinite time, done so.)

Nevertheless, we are faced with a basic choice which comes down to: if our current universe started at the Big Bang from a very tiny something or other, something about the size of a pea or even smaller, what were things like before that point in time? Was there simply nothing or was there a prior 'universe', one which perhaps collapsed on itself to form that pea-sized entity? And note that <u>science can't answer that question for us</u>. It does not (and cannot) have access to any empirical data that might have existed prior to that time.

In addition, there is this consideration:

> "There could be no such thing as a first event, *looked at from a strictly physical perspective*. If things had to begin . . . (a big bang?) the question is, "Why only then, why not earlier?" The answer has to be: "Conditions were not yet right." What was it for "conditions to become right"? Something had to happen first (i.e. before the big bang). Thus there is always an event presupposed by any posited "first event." The big bang, even if it is science and not mere "literary conception," is only an interesting event." [emph. mine]
> Lawrence Dewan,
> *"Big Bang, If There Was One, Was No Big Deal,"*
> New York Times, 7 May, 1990

In this chapter, however, we are focusing on the case where the physical universe does have an absolute beginning, where it is conceived of as coming into being from a state where there was no prior existing matter or matter-energy dyad.

2) And our question then is: *why* did it do so? This question itself is very revealing and uncovers what is perhaps the most basic principle behind our understanding of anything. For the question implies that **we think <u>there must be</u> *some* reason/cause for whatever happens**. It implies that to achieve understanding, we require that we come to know the cause, or the reason(s), for what has happened. We're convinced that things don't just happen for no reason at all. Or if they seem to have, we consider that to be an as yet unexplained fact. Something which currently escapes our understanding. This is huge! This principle is usually referred to as **the principle of sufficient reason** and can be stated in this way:

> For whatever happens, there must be some reason (cause)
> for why it happened and for why it is what it is.

As it stands, this principle is ambiguous, but in a very rich way. Is it referring to the way 'things' are and must be, or is it referring to what is required for us to consider that we *understand* anything? Does it govern reality or only what our understanding anything requires? In the first case, we'd call it a metaphysical principle, a principle which governs the way 'things' *must* be. In the second case, we'd call it an epistemological principle, what is required for us to claim that we *know* or understand something, anything. In the rest of this chapter, I'll be focusing on this second way of looking at the principle. Though it should be noted that when we claim to *know* anything, to understand anything, we assume that what we know or understand about X is so because that's the way X really is.

Why such a principle is demanded for our understanding anything can best be seen by considering its alternative. The alternative would be: "no reason, it just randomly, and for no reason at all, occurred." And faced with that 'answer', our minds go blank. Things just occur for no reason at all? That totally stymies any understanding. Science, e.g., would not be possible if that were the case. Even in situations where we don't know the cause of something, e.g. why photons / other entities pop into and out of existence in otherwise empty interstellar space, we assume there must be *some* reason or explanation. We just haven't found it yet. So this principle of sufficient reason underlies our search for understanding and therefore also, for all of science.

In addition to being a metaphysical principle then, a principle that governs the way 'things' are or must be, it is also a principle of rationality and understanding. A statement that points out what it is to understand something, to understand anything at all.

3) Well, then, back to our original question: *why* did the universe begin? As we've just seen, the theory of **The Big Bang** does not answer this "why?" It may answer a "how?" or a "when?", but even then, not for any absolute beginning since the big bang may just be the starting point for this particular cycle.

One reason that has been offered, but one which is not so much an answer to "why?" as it is stipulating that there is no answer or, at least, that we can't find any. And that answer is: 'Ooops! And there it was.' In effect, this is saying that there is no reason, it just happened. We have no idea why because there is no reason why. It's a purely chance event.

But note that to say: we have no idea why, is quite different from saying that there is no why, no reason at all for its coming into existence, that it is purely and only a random, a surd event. And this last 'answer' might even be taken a step further by saying: 'there is no reason (no cause) at all, *and none is needed.*' But I would respond that such an answer amounts to nothing more than: we must give up any hope of understanding *why* the universe began. It just did, period. End of story.

An alternative answer that has been given to our original question is: **creation**. This answer assumes that something non-physical, not composed of matter and energy can exist. Consciousness or intelligence (Mind) are often considered to be just such 'things'. And, of course, whatever it is, it must not be part of the universe as we are conceiving it, for then it would exist before it existed, which is nonsense. So it is not composed of matter and energy but can create matter and energy.

What does that mean exactly? What does it mean to "create" in this sense? It means to be able to bring something into being out of nothing. Or, perhaps more accurately, to bring something physical out of something non-physical. And perhaps the creations of an artist or an engineer or a chemist can stand as analogues for such creation. The artist has an idea of something they would like to create, a painting perhaps, and from that non-physical idea they create something physical. The difference, of course, is that in the case of the artist, they are using materials that already exist, whereas in the case of the creation of the universe, the materials did not already exist, they had to be made.

It's not, then, how can you (anyone) make something out of nothing so much as how can anyone make something physical out of something non-physical? Can a combination of intention, intelligence and power explain it? Perhaps. Perhaps not. (See Ch. 9 below.) But it does, it seems to me, make it thinkable. It takes it out of the realm of the **im**possible.

Are there other possibilities? Other answers to the: *why* did the universe begin? Let's review.

- It didn't (the universe is cyclical and has always been).

- There is no reason at all, it just did (Ooops!). (Contrary to the principle of sufficient reason).
- Creation
- There is no reason that we can discover. Perhaps because some intelligence willed that it come into being for reasons we can only guess at. (Unless you get into the whole area of revelation which we will not be doing here.)

Which answer strikes <u>you</u> as the most plausible?

4) Arguments from authority won't work in this area any more than they do elsewhere, but here are some provocative, short, comments you might find of interest regarding our question:

> "It is enough for me to contemplate the mystery of conscious life perpetuating itself through all eternity, to reflect upon the marvelous structure of the universe which we dimly perceive, and to try humbly to *comprehend an infinitesimal part of the intelligence manifested in nature.*" [emph. mine]
>
> Albert Einstein
>
> Something exists now, so something must always have existed.
>   (Because you can't get something from nothing.)
> And we have a choice, we can decide that that something which has always existed is matter (today, we'd probably say: the matter-energy dyad), or it's intelligence.
> To me, intelligence seems the much more likely candidate.
>
> Paraphrase of an argument by
Cardinal John Henry Newman

(Einstein and Cardinal Newman, . . . not too shabby.)

But this was **not** the point of this chapter. Rather, the point was: what lies behind the question about why did the universe begin. And what lies behind it is **that principle of sufficient reason**. The cornerstone for our understanding anything. The conviction that things don't just happen for no reason at all. The conviction that to understand something *entails that* we know why it has occurred and why it is what it is.

Ken Wilber captures this conviction quite nicely when he says:

> "It is FLAT-OUT strange that something–that *anything*– is happening at all. There was nothing, then a Big Bang, then here we all are. This is extremely weird.
>
> To Schelling's burning question, "Why is there something rather than nothing?," there have always been two general answers. The first might be called the philosophy of "oops." The universe just occurs, there is nothing behind it, it's all ultimately accidental or random, it just is, it just happens– oops! The philosophy of oops, no matter how sophisticated and adult it may on occasion appear– its modern names and numbers are legion, from positivism to scientific materialism, from linguistic analysis to historical materialism, from naturalism to empiricism– always comes down to the same basic answer, namely, "Don't ask."
>
> The question itself (Why is anything at all happening? Why am I here?)– the *question itself* is said to be confused, pathological, nonsensical, or infantile. To stop asking such silly or confused questions is, they all maintain, the mark of maturity, the sign of growing up in this cosmos. I don't think so. I think the "answer" these "modern and mature"

disciplines give–namely, oops! (and therefore, "Don't ask!")– is about as infantile a response as the human condition could possibly offer.

The other broad answer that has been tendered is that *something else is going on*: behind the happenstance drama is a deeper or higher or wider pattern, or order, or intelligence. There are, of course, many varieties of this "Deeper Order": the Tao, God, Geist, Maat, Archetypal Forms, Reason, Li, Mahamaya, Brahman, Rigpa. And although these different varieties of the Deeper Order certainly disagree with each other at many points, they all agree on this: the universe is not what it appears. *Something else* is going on, something quite other than oops. . . ."

> Ken Wilber
> from the Introduction to his
> *Sex, Ecology and Spirituality,* revised edition.

****

Thus, to say that "it just is" or "it just did" in response to a question about what something is or why it occurred, yields no understanding at all, it simply calls a halt to the questioning. Whereas understanding anything requires making / seeing the connections, the relationships, that enable that thing to come into being and to be what it is.

Seeing the connections that explain how the outcome you're focused on has come to be.

"Ooops!" does not do this. In fact, it pretty explicitly says either that there are no such connections or that we can't discover what they might be. In either case, understanding would not be possible because no connections are being alleged.

Any endeavor to understand anything is looking precisely for just such connections, whether it's in the empirical sciences or psychological therapy or art, music and literature or theology.

Chapter Outline   **Chapter 9**

Dear Dalai Lama

1. The universe and our experience of matter and consciousness within it leads to a puzzle. . . . .
(The propositions behind the puzzle: matter and spirit are not the same <u>and</u> one cannot become the other.) The more common, the more usual, way this conundrum is presented:
            Quote from the Dalai Lama.

2. Here, we'll turn the question "on its head." . . . → how can something material come from something <u>non</u>-material?
Does **a negative answer** (i.e. "it cannot") to the question we've just put to the Dalai Lama inevitably lead us back to some form of **dualism**? (Spirit and Matter, e.g.) Explain.
It would seem to. (If there are both and one cannot come from the other, then . . . .)
This "solution", however, seems to relegate the material to some kind of second-class status.

3. But there is another possibility. Namely, a dualism *as we experience the world* and thus the material world is very "real" in that sense. And a dualism of the <u>dependent</u> and the <u>non</u>-dependent (Ch. 6, above). But a monism of the non-dependent. (Only one thing can be such and everything that exists does depend on that non-dependent entity or being.)

4. But is this 'solution' **just a restatement of the Two Truths doctrine** of Buddhism? And we found problems with that in Ch. 7 (above). But "no," because this understanding does not fall into a self-contradiction (of being both a dualism and a monism at the same time and in the same way) since the dualism and the monism here are not so <u>in the same way</u>.

5. This answer, however, still does not tell us *how* consciousness / intelligence (the immaterial) can give rise to the material. Alas, that may be "above our pay-grade."

Chapter 9
Dear Dalai Lama

1) Our experience of the world around us and of each other, leads to a puzzle. And that puzzle has many expressions. For example, what is the relationship between the mind and the brain? Or what is the relationship between matter and spirit, or between matter and consciousness? And it's a puzzle because the two realities referred to definitely do not seem to be the same *kind* of thing and we don't see how one can become the other. Here's how the Dalai Lama expressed this puzzle.

> "We [Buddhists] say that consciousness is produced from consciousness. Consciousness must be produced from consciousness because it cannot be produced with matter as its substantial cause. Particles cannot create an entity of luminosity and knowing. Matter cannot be the substantial cause of consciousness . . . . There is no way to posit consciousness except as being a continuation of former moments of consciousness; in this way consciousness can have no beginning . . ."
>
> Dalai Lama
> *Kindness, Clarity and Insight*, p. 76

In contemporary Western philosophy, a very similar dilemma has become known as "the hard problem" and its contemporary expression was first (?) formulated by David Chalmers. Here is part of a commentary on this from Wikipedia.

> "The hard problem, in contrast, is the problem of why and how those [brain] processes are accompanied by experience. . . . In other words, the hard problem is the

problem of explaining why certain mechanisms are accompanied by conscious experience. For example, why should neural processing in the brain lead to the felt sensations of, say, feelings of hunger? And why should those neural firings lead to feelings of hunger rather than some other feeling (such as, for example, feelings of thirst)?"

"Chalmers argues that it is conceivable that the relevant behaviors associated with hunger, or any other feeling, could occur even in the absence of that feeling. *This suggests that experience is irreducible to physical systems such as the brain.*" (emph. mine)

And finally, here is an expression of the problem from a still different perspective, but one which nicely captures the puzzle. The speaker here is Roland Griffiths, a scientist at Johns Hopkins who has been studying the effects of psychedelics on various health problems for over 20 years.

"No, I can easily inhabit an evolutionary account that explains how we have come to be who we are —*with the exception of the question of interiority*! Why would evolution waste its precious energy on our having interior experiences at all? I don't get that. To me, it's a very precious mystery, and that mystery, if you want to put it in religious terms, is God. It's the unknowable. It's unfathomable. I don't believe in God as conceptualized within different religious traditions, but the mystery thing is something that strikes me as undeniable." [Emph. mine]

A Psychedelics Pioneer Takes the Ultimate Trip
By David Marchese
https://www.nytimes.com/interactive/2023/04/03/magazine/roland-griffiths-interview.html

For our purposes in the remainder of this chapter, I'm going to focus on the Dalai Lama's comment above. (Hence, the title of the chapter.)

2) And I'll start by turning his point "on its head" so-to-speak. He says that according to Buddhist doctrine, consciousness cannot be produced by/from matter. The two are just so different that there is no way matter could give rise to mind/consciousness. But then, how can it go the other way? How can consciousness give rise to matter as it would have to do if it (consciousness or anything wholly immaterial, e.g. God) was the cause of anything material?

We do have experience of how consciousness or mind (thought, ideas) can give rise to, can create all sorts of things. Artists, engineers, mathematicians, poets, musical composers, all of these create stuff, much of it in a material form, from something purely mental, from ideas, imagination and concepts. BUT, in all of these cases they need something material, from canvas and paint to marble to mathematical symbols to musical notes, to building materials to bring their imagined creation to physical reality. So, yes, they create something material from something immaterial (ideas, etc.) but to actually make the thing created different from something purely mental, they must have physical materials to work with.

So that example won't solve our problem. How can something *purely immaterial* create something material? If, as the Dalai Lama claims, it can't go from material to immaterial, from matter to consciousness, how can it go the other way?

3) Dualism as a solution? But does it, paradoxically, lead back to a monism?

Wouldn't it be easiest to just say that ultimately, **reality is dualistic**? There is matter and there is spirit or the non-material; there is brain and there is mind or consciousness; the dependent and the non-dependent. And the one doesn't come from the other.

It would be easier. Except for that last dichotomy. There, the very meaning of the terms raises problems. The dependent depends, by definition, on something, namely, on the non-dependent. And that would seem to imply that *ultimately*, there is just one thing, the non-dependent. And everything else comes from and depends on that. So *ultimately*, we have a monism of that which exists in and of itself; of that which exists necessarily.

One problem with this 'solution' is that it seems to reduce the material world to something not real or, maybe, something not "really real" and that flies in the face of how we experience our lives and the world we live in. We interact with and live in and through this dependent reality all the time. From the people we love to whatever we might accomplish, from the mundane to the exotic, it all involves this so-called dependent reality. So calling it "not real" or not "really real" just seems totally absurd.

Is there any way to resolve this dilemma? Perhaps this: both the dependent and the non-dependent exist, both are real (though in different ways) and that supports the dualism of our experience. But there is a relationship of dependence of one on the other so that it can be said that *ultimately* there is just one thing (the non-dependent) and everything else ultimately depends on that one thing (and *in that sense*, monism prevails). At the level of how we experience things, a dualism. At the level of how we explain and understand the most basic relationship(s) between 'things', a monism.

And why would we say that ultimately it's a monism of the *non-material*? I assume that reasoning would look something like this: matter and consciousness both exist. One of them, matter, is something that is composed (has parts) and anything that is composed is something that can become de-composed or go out of existence. But consciousness is not composed and therefore cannot become de-composed and cannot, at least in that way, go out of existence. Further, anything that is composed is contingent or <u>dependent</u>. (It is, at least, dependent upon its parts.) And anything that is not-composed is not contingent or dependent. So anything and everything that exists <u>dependently</u>, must ultimately depend upon something that does not exist dependently. So if matter exists, it must depend upon something non-material, and that something is consciousness (intelligence / Mind?). Hence the material, if it has not always existed, comes from the immaterial, the dependent from the non-dependent and that which exists contingently from that which exists necessarily. But this still doesn't answer the question of ***how*** the one can come from the other?

The Dalai Lama's answer to the question of how can consciousness come from matter was to say that it can't and it didn't. Rather, it already was, indeed, it has always existed.

Well then, what about matter? Could it also always existed? The theory of a Big Bang, as we saw in the previous chapter, need not rule out matter as having always existed since it does not rule out a cyclical universe. But there are other considerations that do seem to rule out matter as having always existed. **Entropy** is one. If matter is convertible into energy (E=mc^2), and ultimately there will be no energy, doesn't that entail that ultimately there will be no matter?

Contingency is an even stronger argument. If something is contingent, it is dependent upon something else for its continuing existence. And anything composed is contingent. But everything material is something that is composed. So everything material is something that is contingent. And so it would seem that matter must have been (and must be?) created at some point. But *how* can that be? If matter and consciousness are as different as the Dali Lama claims (in the quote at the beginning of this chapter), so that matter cannot cause (create) consciousness, how can consciousness cause (create) matter? I don't know *how*.

Well then, what does this mean, if anything, for one of the earlier issues we raised: the issue of monism vs. dualism? We seem to have come down to: matter and the spiritual (e.g. consciousness) are two very different kinds of 'things', hence there is a dualism. But ultimately, anything material comes from (and depends on?) consciousness or intelligence or . . . (something immaterial), and *in that sense*, monism reigns. There is just one 'thing' that is not conditioned, not contingent, and everything else depends on that one thing. Soooo, we arrive at a more complex answer. *Ultimately*, there is only one 'thing' that is not composed or is unconditioned (and is, therefore, immaterial) and everything else comes from and depends on that one thing. In that sense and to that degree, reality is a monism. BUT, there really are objects ('things') which are material, interrelated (but not dependent upon most other material things *for their existence)*, and which exist independently of our thinking of them. In that sense, and to that degree, the world, the universe, reality, is dualistic.

So, reality is both dualistic and monistic? Yes. **But not** at the same level or in the same way. As lived in our daily existence and in terms of the nature of things, it's dualistic. As existing either dependently or non-dependently, it is dualistic. But as existing non-dependently, not conditioned, there is only one 'thing'. And that one thing must be that from which all else comes. *In that sense*, reality is a monism.

4) But doesn't this, then, just take us back to something like the Two Truths Doctrine which we found reasons for rejecting in chapter seven? Perhaps so, but now understood in a different way.

We argued earlier that the Two Truths Doctrine entailed a dualism (of the dependent and the not-dependent) not a monism of Buddha-Nature or Consciousness. Here we are affirming that kind of dualism but saying that the unreality, the illusoriness, which the Two Truths Doctrine attributed to the things of the world goes too far. They are, ultimately, dependent, but not illusory.

So which is it??! Is the world, the universe, everything that exists, ultimately a monism or a dualism? In terms of what and how we experience and of how we understand reality, it's a dualism. In terms of dependence and non-dependence, it is a dualism. But in terms of what does and can exist non-dependently, it is a monism, only one thing can do so. **Why?** If X exists non-dependently, it exists in and of itself; it cannot not exist or it exists necessarily. But if there were two 'things' which existed necessarily, whose very essence was to exist, there would be no way of distinguishing one from the other so they would, in the final analysis, be identical. (Cf. Leibniz's law.)

5) And note that traditional religions which profess belief in God as *the creator* of the universe don't know *how* either. They simply fall back onto something like: God is all powerful and can do anything that is not logically impossible. Creating matter out of nothing is not logically impossible, so God can do it. *How* God does it, is "above our pay-grade."

Answer the Dalai Lama might now give to our question: *How can consciousness (something nonphysical) give rise to the physical?*

1. It doesn't. They both exist from forever. No. He wouldn't and doesn't say this. It would be inconsistent with some things being <u>d</u>ependent.)
2. We don't know *how*, but *we reason that* <u>it does</u> on the grounds that consciousness or the non-dependent, non-material must have always been (cannot not be) and hence is the only source possible for the dependent, the physical. Still, no answer as to *how*, but a definite answer ***that*** it does.

Chapter Outline   **Chapter 10**

Why be kind?   (Cf. Bk.1, Ch. 3 & Bk.2, Ch.10)

1) Whatever is/ may be true at the metaphysical level, (whether anything spiritual exists, e.g.), this: be kind to others / love your neighbor, certainly seems to be 'true' on the lived level. I.e. we take it as accurately describing what is in fact *the right way* to *live*. (True *in that sense*.) Indeed, isn't it *the touchstone* we use (and should use) to test *any* religion or moral philosophy?
   I.e. any alleged religious claim that would not at least support / be consistent with this view, we would think is a false claim.
   Virtually every religion and most secularists would agree that being kind to one another is the way one should live one's life.
   The Dalai Lama, e.g., has been quoted as saying: . . . .

2) But *WHY* should one be kind?   (Cf. Bk.1, Ch. 3)
Is it **all just transactional**? I.e., & basically, just (enlightened) self-interest? E.g. something like:
   'If I act in this way, 1) I'm more likely to be treated in this same way by others.' Or
   'If I act in this way, 2) there's a better chance that the world will turn out as *I* want it to'.
Or is there some genuinely *moral imperative* to it?
   "Moral imperative"? . . . .
   (1) The Gyges challenge, from long ago, seems to raise this question. (Cf. Bk. 3, p. 44)
   (2) And cf. Vaclav Havel's claim about something or someone always watching . . . .
       But, . . . merely indicative, not demonstrative in either case.
   (3) Francis Collins & C. S. Lewis think there is and that such a felt moral imperative may also be the (only?) way a God could indicate his/her presence to us.   (See Ch. 3, above.)

3) In addition, this moral imperative seems **inherently connected to harming or helping other people** which itself raises the question of what is to count as such?

4) And that, in turn, is tied to the further issue of whether there is something that it is to be a "fully realized human being" or is that a purely arbitrary and idiosyncratic choice on the part of each individual?

Chapter 10
Why be Kind?

1) Whatever is true at the metaphysical level, this: be kind to others / love your neighbor, certainly seems to be true in the moral realm. (True *in that sense*.) Indeed, isn't it *the* touchstone we use (or should use) to test any so-called moral claim? I.e. if any religion or moral philosophy would not at least support / be consistent with this view, then we deem it to very likely be mistaken. Virtually every religion and most secularists would agree that being kind to one another is the way one *should* live one's life. The Dalai Lama, e.g., has been quoted as saying: "Kindness is my religion."

Consider the difference, however, between being kind simply because that's the way you would like to be and to be treated yourself and being kind ("loving one another"?) because that's the way you think you *ought* to be. The first is simply a personal preference. You or someone else might not feel or hold that preference at all. And that would be all right. Almost like a matter of taste. The second is experienced as **an obligation**, something we (each and all of us) *ought* to do. I take it that the Dalai Lama, in the above, quote, was referring to something more like the latter. It's what he believes in as the way one *should* live one's life. At least, that's the way I'll be taking it for the sake of this essay.

2) And then one can ask: but *why*? **Why** should one behave in that way? Is it **all just transactional**? I.e., basically, just self-interest? Albeit, perhaps, "enlightened" self-interest. E.g. something like: if I act in this way,

1. I'm more likely to be treated in this way by others. Or if I act in this way,
2. there's a better chance that the world will turn out <u>as I want it</u> to. Or
3. if I act in this way, I'll go to heaven and avoid going to hell. Or is there some genuinely *moral imperative* to it? Is it *the morally right* way to live? And what would that even mean, "*the morally right* way to live"?

I would like to consider, briefly, three different examples which will, hopefully, help us to fill in this notion of *a morally right* way to live, or the notion of a *moral obligation* at all. **The first** comes from Plato, **the second** is a simple quote from Vaclav Havel and **the third** refers to an experience that Francis Collins (the former head of the National Institutes of Health) writes of in recounting his own sojourn from atheism to theism.

In the second book of Plato's *Republic*, Plato has Glaucon relate a mythical story about a shepherd named Gyges, who finds a magical ring which allows him to become invisible. (Do you think maybe Tolkien (*The Lord of the Rings*) had read his Plato?) Glaucon uses the story of Gyges to illustrate a cynical (or a more realistic and accurate?) view of morality and moral obligation. For in the story, as Glaucon relates it, Gyges does all sorts of bad and nasty things (seducing a queen, killing her husband, taking over a kingdom, etc.) because he can. The ring gives him the power to do any nasty thing he pleases *without any negative consequences* for himself. And as Glaucon sees it, that's the only reason that, people do "the right thing." They fear the negative consequences that are likely to befall them if they are caught doing something "wrong," something "evil". So any so-called "moral obligation" is really just a name we've invented for acting in ways that will avoid harm to our own reputation or life. It's all merely and purely a transactional thing. In effect, any "moral obligation" is nothing over and above that self-serving strategy. And that's exactly what we are inquiring about here, is there any such thing as *moral obligation* or is it all just enlightened self-interest?

Vaclav Havel was an author, poet, playwright and dissident, and then president of Czechoslovakia and the Czech Republic in the latter part of the 20th century. And in one of his writings, he said:

> ".... there is a 'higher' responsibility, which grows out of a conscious or subconscious certainty that our death ends nothing, because everything is forever being recorded and evaluated somewhere else, somewhere 'above us' in . . . an integral aspect of the secret order of the cosmos, of nature, and of life, which believers call God and to whose judgment everything is liable."
>
> – Vaclav Havel

I quote this here not as proof or evidence of anything other than Havel's conviction that what we feel or experience as a *moral obligation* is based on something more and other than a simple transactional worldview. Rather, he sees it as grounded in some conception or awareness that this world, this life, is not all there is. That there is a greater context in which we live and move and have our being and in that greater context, certain ways of behaving are deemed more consonant with the structure and design both of ourselves and of the universe, and therefore are expected of us.

Yes, yes, but still, might this not be construed now simply as a form of 'enlightened' self-interest? I.e. any so-called "obligation" is still based on a quid-pro-quo, it's just that the "quo" may not occur until after one's death. Whether it's this-worldly consequences (the story of Gyges) or some other worldly consequences (Havel's "somewhere 'above us'"), isn't it still simply transactional? Is there anything other and different from this that constitutes what we feel and analyze as a *moral obligation*?

Most religions seem to have adopted a Havel-like view. Whether it's the heaven and hell of the Abrahamic religions or the Karma and re-birth of the Eastern religions, our felt moral obligation is tied to positive or negative consequences for us, either here or hereafter. And yet that doesn't seem to fully capture the sense of obligation *as we experience it*. It's not a matter of doing this to get that, it's something more like: this is the right way to act, and not acting in this way rejects or denies our truest nature. It rejects or denies how we *should* try to be. Now, can we capture *this sense* of moral obligation without appealing to God? Perhaps not.

Francis Collins, in his book: *The Language of God*, speaks of this as one of the pivotal moments in his own journey from atheism to theism. In doing so, he references C. S. Lewis's book *Mere Christianity*. In that book, Lewis argues that this felt obligation to act or not act in certain ways, call it the moral law, is something real. It really exists even though it doesn't do so in the same way that a stone really exists. Indeed, he claims that it is something that everyone, all humans everywhere and throughout time, have experienced. Lewis then goes on to argue that such a felt, universal *obligation* must have come from "a controlling power outside the universe."

Though he cautions:

> "Do not think I am going faster than I really am. I am not yet within a hundred miles of the God of Christian theology. All I have got to is a Something which is directing the universe, and which appears in me as a law urging me to do right and making me feel responsible and uncomfortable when I do wrong. I think we have to assume it is more like a mind than it is like anything else we know– because after all the only other thing we know is matter and you can hardly imagine a bit of matter giving instructions."
>
> C. S. Lewis
Mere Christianity, p. 25

Whether Lewis's argument that such a universally felt obligation must have come from "a controlling power outside the universe" I'll leave to the reader to investigate on their own. But it convinced Collins that Lewis was right that this universally felt moral law was indeed a way (and perhaps the only possible way) that a God, if there was such, could "show" or reveal him/herself.

> "The only way in which we could expect it to show itself would be inside ourselves as an influence or a command trying to get us to behave in a certain way. And that is just what we do find inside ourselves."
>
> Ibid., p. 24

And so, <u>this answer</u> to our original question: "*Why* be kind?" apparently comes down to: because there is a law or at least a conviction within us that this way of acting is required and expected of us IF we are going to live as we *should*. That there is another realm in addition to the purely physical realm that characterizes and governs our lives, call it **the moral realm**, and this realm also has its laws (just as the physical realm does). The difference: planets <u>have to</u> act the way they do, whereas humans are *obligated* to act in certain ways IF they want to live as they should, but they do not <u>have to</u> act in those ways.

Collins takes this 'fact' as evidence for the existence of God but we are not looking at it in that way here. Rather, we were trying to discover if there is some reason other than self-interest for treating others with kindness. <u>Is</u> it all simply a matter of a <u>quid pro quo</u>, of 'I'll treat you in this way so that you'll treat me similarly' or is there something more to it? When the Dalai Lama speaks of it as being his "religion" is he just being an Eastern Dale Carnegie (*How to Make Friends and Influence People*) or is he pointing to something deeper?

Is it the case that there actually is such a thing as a *moral obligation*? *A felt imperative* to act or not act in certain ways. If Lewis is right (and consult your own experience to check that), there is.

3) From somewhere and somehow there is a universally felt sense that certain ways of behaving are *morally* wrong or *morally* right and that we are *obligated* on those grounds to avoid doing the former and engage in doing the latter. And that such obligation is not based on any <u>quid-pro-quo</u> strategy but seems to come from the very nature of the actions themselves, our connection to all other humans and something in the way the universe is structured. These sorts of activities just are the sorts of things that *ought* to be done or *ought* to be eschewed. And usually (always?) the former are such that they help other people and the latter are such that they harm other people. Thus what we feel obligated to do or to avoid doing is essentially connected to what helps or harms other people.

4) And that, "what helps or harms other people" then leaves us with the question of what counts as helping or harming another person? **Is there a way that people can be or become which captures what it is to be "a fully realized human being"** and thus whatever hinders them from becoming such "harms" them and whatever enables their becoming such "helps" them?

It is hard to overstate the centrality and importance of the question above in bold since so much else depends on how we answer it. From what each of us is (or should be?) trying to do in and with our own lives? To what is truly valuable or worthwhile in human existence? To our current subject: what counts as harming or helping other persons? And this latter not only defines our morality, but is (or should be?) what underlies our social structure and our system of laws.

An oft repeated instance or example of how and where this distinction impacts our lives is the so-called "Hippocratic oath." "First, do no harm," is relatively easy to abide by in the context of our bodies and their physical health. But determining what counts as "no harm" more generally can be much more tricky and difficult when dealing in the areas of mental well-being or attaining skills or education and especially, character development. Both because the results are often harder to measure and because they often take time to emerge.

Nevertheless, having an idea of what counts as "a fully realized human being" gives us direction and a standard for determining "harm" and "help" to other humans in our lives (and even to ourselves?) And if avoiding harm and doing good underlies the most basic of our moral obligations, having this sort of direction is immeasurably helpful.

Chapter Outline   **Chapter 11**

**Must there be a lasting and good end-state for our
lives to be meaningful and valuable?**

1. **Meanings of "end-state": A (merely) notional concept. . . or an eventual, actual reality?**
    Two different ways of conceiving of an end-state: as a mosaic or as a black hole.

2. **Why might one think that there must be a lasting and good end-state?**
    (1) If the end-state of the world / universe would be exactly the same with or without your life, with or without your existence, then your existence has made no difference, and if it has made no difference, then it has been of no significance.
       (1.1) There is no difference that doesn't make a difference....
    (2) Because of its place in **a particular worldview** -
    The worldview in question: what gives our lives meaning and value is that they do make a difference in and to the final outcome.
    (3) Based on the belief that the world is lawful in the moral realm as it is in the physical realm.

3. **But is it even possible that your life make no difference at all??**
    No. Or, at least, it's virtually impossible. If your life makes a difference in the here-and-now, then it makes a difference. The argument at (1) above begged the question. It assumed . . . Must we conclude, then, that **the worldview** *as described above* **is wrong**? Whatever and to whomever your life makes a difference, THAT is what makes it valuable and significant, **not** that any difference it has made is represented in some substantial end-state.

4. Ahhhh, **BUT**, does the difference your life has made have to be a "good" difference for your life to have meaning and value? Or will it still be meaningful and valuable even if the difference(s) you've made are, on balance, destructive, damaging and harmful? Compare, e.g., the Dalai Lama vs. Pol Pot, Sister Theresa vs. Stalin, or Mahatma Gandhi vs. Hitler.

Chapter 11
Must there be a lasting and good end-state for our lives to have meaning and value?

What is even meant by an "end-state" here? What is being imagined is a state-of-affairs in which all humans have perished from the earth, there is no more human life on earth or anywhere in the universe. There is another end-state, of course, namely that in which all the energy in the universe has decreased to a zero level or the final end-state resulting from entropy: "the degradation of the matter and energy in the universe to an ultimate state of inert uniformity." But since the second entails the first, I am going to focus on the first of these end-states.

No more human life anywhere in the universe is quite easily imaginable and certainly possible. In fact, my guess is that virtually everyone who has thought about this would also say that it is not just possible but that it is probable. Perhaps even, a certainty. Especially in today's world.

But a clarification needs to be made. When I say "there is no more human life anywhere in the universe" I mean in *the physical universe* as we now know it. I do <u>not</u> mean "anywhere, everywhere and any how." Indeed, <u>that</u> is actually a presumption behind this question. <u>Is there</u>, will there be, any human consciousness anywhere after all humans are physically gone from the earth (and any other planet if we happen to colonize such)? And further, <u>must</u> there be such an end-state and must any such final state be good in order for our lives in the here and now to have had meaning and value?

This is not focusing on any personal heaven (though it can include that). Rather it's focus is on the end-state after all human life has perished on earth. And the question heading this chapter is asking whether such an end-state needs to be both lasting and good in order for our lives in the here and now to have had meaning and value.

Before proceeding any further, we need to clarify the kind of end-state we are imagining or talking about here. There are at least two different ways of conceiving what such an end-state might look like. In one way, such an end-state may be thought of as a finished work of art, for example a large Jackson Pollack painting, or a large and complex mosaic. In each of these cases, every little dot and dribble of paint or every little piece of stone or colored glass, contributes to the resulting work of art. Each little bit or piece does make a difference in the final outcome. It might be hard to discern what the difference is, but we know that it is making *some* difference in the overall effect of that painting or mosaic on its viewers.

Now, imagine another kind of end-state. Consider a black hole. A space where the gravity is so great that everything nearby is sucked into the black hole, even nearby light. So far as we can determine, there is simply nothing "inside" such a black hole, just . . . nothing. So anything that has gotten sucked into the black hole has made absolutely no difference to its being now. It's just a big, black, hole with nothing at the bottom, so to speak. Or we could consider the heat death of the universe. There is not enough heat energy left anywhere in the universe for that energy to be converted into anything positive.

2) Why in heaven's name would one ever think that there must be a good and lasting end-state for our lives in the here-and-now to have meaning and value? There are at least **three possible reasons** one might think that. In **the first**, the reasoning in support of such a view might go something like this:

(1) **if** the end-state (for you and for the cosmos) would be exactly the same whether or not <u>you</u> had ever lived, then your life has not made any difference.
And if your life has not made <u>any</u> difference, then it has been of absolutely no significance and has had no meaning or value. This kind of view depends on the claim that:
"there is no difference that doesn't make a difference."

And **the second** reason one might think of to support the claim that there must be a good and lasting end-state has to do with a particular world view. The worldview that **a good and loving God** exists. How would this lead to a particular conception of, a particular vision of, an end-state? E.g. that of a complex mosaic in which each life contributes something to the overall reality, the overall effect, of that end-state. And here, the thinking might go as follows:

(2) our lives are creating a tapestry, a mosaic composed of everything that we think and do and feel. Some of it good, some of it bad, and some merely neutral. And in this effort we are actually joined with God in the creation of the world. A good and loving God would not want to simply, as it were, dump all this effort and 'product' into a trash bin of nothingness. But He/She/It would want it to continue to exist as *somehow* a part of whatever does exist.

The key to this argument, of course, is this: a good and loving God would not want to simply, as it were, dump all this effort and product into a trash bin of nothingness. That does seem to be a reasonable expectation of a good and loving God. The problem, of course, is that the argument depends on the premise that such a being actually does exist and that premise itself is so open to question as to not be of much help in establishing any answer to our question about what kind of end-state will, in fact, prevail.

It paints a pretty picture to be sure, nice imaginings, and maybe even a legitimate depiction of what a good and loving God *would or would not* do, but it could also be nothing more than wishful thinking.

> (3) And there is yet a third reason or set of reasons for thinking that the final end-state would not be a black- hole-like nothing. This reason reflects **the belief that the universe is lawful in the moral realm** as it is in the physical realm. See Bk. 1, Ch. 3

Consider the way we experience any (and all?) moral obligations /claims on our actions. It is felt or believed that there is or should be *some* negative consequence(s) for the actor if he/she acts immorally. Those consequences may not occur in the here-and-now or even in the relatively near future, but they will be suffered at some point. For example: it might be thought that they affect or help form one's character and *that* has some lasting affect, as in "character is destiny." Ultimately, it is believed (hoped?) that you "don't get away with" anything. But for that to be the case, there would have to be some form of afterlife in which justice would prevail since, so far as we can see, there are clearly instances of people "getting away with" evil in the here-and-now, in this life. I.e., they commit some evil deed and, as far as we can tell, there are no negative consequences visited upon them, ever. Or at least no negative consequences comparable to the evil they have done or to the unnecessary suffering they have caused.

This could stand, then, as an additional explanation for how one gets to an end-state more like a complex mosaic, viz. from the demands of morality. In that view of an end-state, what you do now, how you live now, <u>does</u> have an effect on the final outcome.

3) "Wait, wait, wait" I can hear you saying. "Your reasoning *assumes* that unless there is some *lasting forever* effect of your life, your decisions, actions, effects of those actions, character, etc., then your life has had no meaning or value. But that's crazy! What about the effects its had in the here-and-now and on the people with whom you've lived and loved and possibly even those beyond that circle of known others? Clearly your life has had some effect on them. And wouldn't that be enough to give it meaning and value? (Depending on the effect its had?) Why would there be any need for some end-state to give it meaning and value? Your claim that if your life has made no difference to the end-state, then your life has made no difference at all (argument at (1) above) simply begs this question." (You're right, it does.) "But such an end-state (the mosaic kind) would not be necessary for your life to have meaning and value. That, as we have just seen, could easily be supplied by what you do, how you live, in the here and now."

We can still ask, of course,: which of these different kinds of end-states actually obtains *in relation to our human lives?* And does it make any difference when judging the meaning and value of those lives? Our lives as part of a complex, multifaceted whole which can be considered beautiful or good, or simply . . . nothing.

It's nice to think in terms of the first, but that can hardly sway the day. Is it required ? Is it required by morality, for example? Is it required by suffering? Is it required if God exists? I.e. by any belief that a good and loving God exists. It seems to me that it *is* required if a loving God exists. But in that case, it would not be necessary for our lives to be meaningful and of value. As we've just seen, the here-and-now can supply that function. But it would be necessary for any belief that a good and loving God exists. And perhaps also if there is a moral law which governed the universe. So perhaps the more forceful argument for a mosaic-like end-state is the one from the universe being lawful in the moral realm which we outlined above.

But neither 'argument' really establishes anything like a necessity. Our lives can have meaning and value simply because of what we do in the here and now. There is no need for their effects to last forever. So, "no," there is no necessity for a lasting and good end-state for our lives to be meaningful and valuable.

4) Ahhhh, BUT, does the difference your life has made have to be a "good" difference for your life to have meaning and value? Or will it still be meaningful and valuable even if the difference(s) you've made are, on balance, destructive, damaging and harmful? Compare, e.g., the Dalai Lama vs. Pol Pot, Mother Theresa vs. Hitler, Mahatma Gandhi vs. Hitler and, on a much smaller scale, Albert Schweitzer vs. Jeffrey Dahmer.

Chapter Outline   **Chapter 12**

With respect to making the world a better place to live, does the religious worldview add anything important to the secular humanist worldview?

1. The religious worldview and the secular humanist worldview: what each is. . . . .

2. And the question then is: does the RS worldview cause its adherent(s) to act any differently than the SH would act when it comes to trying to love others and make the world a better place to live?

   With regard to **the best means** for achieving the desired ends, it would seem not. (At least no more difference here than might occur <u>within</u> either group, within either the SH or the RS group.)

   With regard to **the ends** sought, it would also *seem* not. There would be no differences between them. If X comprises an essential element in becoming a fully realized human being, then it cannot be omitted without falling short of achieving that goal whether for oneself or for others.

3. But <u>there are</u> differences between them. Both in how they conceive of the world being a better place to live and in the intentions and motivations behind the actions taken to get there.

   Their differing worldviews
   - (1) The existence or not of **a spiritual realm** and its effects on **how the world's being "a better place to live" is conceived.**
   - (2) Differences in the **intentions and the motivations** driving our actions.
   - (3) The differences resulting from **hope and trust.**
     - Hope and trust that character <u>is</u> destiny. (Refer back to "The One Question" in Ch. 1.)
     - The hope and trust that motivations and intentions do **make a lasting difference**.
     - The hope and trust that in the end, good will prevail.
   - (4) The differences resulting from a different conception of **suffering**.

   Escape from suffering vs. **suffering as redemptive**. What could the latter possibly mean?
   - a.) **It drives home** the commonness of our humanity.
   - b.) It elicits a response of wanting to help (of **loving) the other**.

   And both of these **redeem us** from self-centeredness and selfishness.

   (But, with respect to a.) and b.) (above) couldn't this be equally true for the SH?)

4. Hope and Trust, then <u>would</u> seem to make for a significant difference.

Chapter 12
With respect to making the world a better place to live, does the religious worldview add anything important to the secular humanist worldview?

1) Let's start by trying to describe what each of these two worldviews is or involves. **The secular humanist worldview** (hereafter, the SH worldview) sees (and understands) the world as composed of matter and energy (a materialist conception of things) and that anything over and above those elements, e.g. possibly consciousness, thought, emotions, hopes, fears, etc. depend on that physical / material substrate for their existence and their origin, And this necessary material substrate is usually identified as the brain. In addition, though it would follow from what I've just said, the *secular* humanist rejects anything like a God. (A spiritual, wholly non-material, being which does exist and can act on (indeed, can *create)* and influence material reality.)

But the SH is a **humanist**. He or she firmly believes in the values of truth, beauty and goodness, and thinks that some ways of being a human being are more desirable and noble than are other ways. Humans are, if not perfectible, at least capable of more or less degrees of nobility, open-mindedness, appreciation and enjoyment of beauty in all its many forms, tolerance and caring for others.

The **religious-spiritualist worldview** (hereafter, the RS worldview), can and does accept much of what the SH does, *except* he/she also believes that there does exist a spiritual realm and reality. Something exists which is neither material nor dependent upon the material for its existence and this realm of being includes a God. (In the Abrahamic religions, this being is conceived of as all-powerful, all-knowing, all-good, loving and (the metaphysical part) such that he/she/it cannot not exist, or exists necessarily.)

2) Now the question of this chapter is: when it comes to trying to make the world a better place for humans and all living creatures to live, does the RS worldview add anything of importance to the SH worldview? Would one of these worldviews lead to different sorts of actions or even goals? Or, when it comes to making the world a better place to live, would it be the case that both worldviews would agree on what the final outcome *should* look like and on *how best* to get there?

If there is no difference between them, either in the goals sought or what are considered the best means of achieving those goals, then those considerations could not offer any reason for thinking one worldview to be better than, more likely to be true than, the other. So, it's worth considering.

As we work through trying to find an answer to this question, let's keep in mind, as examples of what would make the world better, such things as: no armed conflicts in the world; respect and dignity afforded to each and every individual irrespective of their race, ethnicity, wealth, position, power and religion. Concern for and attention to the natural environment in which we all live. And a decent standard of living for all. These will be considered as stand-ins for making the world "a better place to live."

So, would the RS act any differently than the SH in trying to achieve these ends? I.e. would they act any differently because of their respective belief systems? At first glance it would seem that the answer would be (must be?) "no". For, IF it's the case that a particular strategy or set of actions is, in fact, **the best means**, the means most likely to achieve a desired end, then anyone interested in achieving that end would, if rational, adopt that strategy. (N.B. for the sake of clarity and simplicity, I am going to ignore the issue of how we arrive at "the best strategy" and the commonly encountered disputes over what any such "best strategy" actually is. Though it's possible that if there is any difference here between the RS and the SH, it may lie in this area, I will set that possibility aside for the moment.)

From a strictly functional viewpoint, then, we would expect both the SH and the RS to adopt that strategy and to do so precisely because it is considered the best strategy for achieving the desired end. (We are assuming that they agree on the desired end in this case– on what it is and *that* it is desired.) So there wouldn't seem to be any difference between the RS and the SH in these instances when it comes to making the world a better place to live, At least none based solely on the metaphysics underlying their respective worldviews.

But what about in **the ends themselves**? Would there by any difference between them there? Would each conceive of the respect and dignity that should be afforded to each and every individual irrespective of their race, ethnicity, wealth, position, power and religion in the same way? I would think so. If one started to explain and defend that goal by saying: "treat all others as you would want to be treated," I would think there would be virtual unanimity among humans on what that "treatment" would look and feel like.

Well then, if there would very likely be agreement on what the ends should be and how they would look, and then also on the best means for achieving those ends, doesn't that then mean that there is no significant difference between the RS and the SH when it comes to making the world a better place to live?

3) Not necessarily. And that is because of two other factors. (1) they may agree on much that would make the world "a better place to live" but not all; and (2) there is an aspect to our actions which is important and which we have not yet considered, viz. the intentions behind and motivating those actions. And I think that once these two factors are accounted for, we'll see that though the RS and the SH can agree on much concerning how to make the world a better place to live, they do not agree on all. Their worldviews are not the same and those differences make a difference. And they make a difference in this area of making the world a better place to live.

Consider (1) above. What would be an example of something that would make the world a better place to live but which the SH and the RS would <u>dis</u>agree on? Pretty obviously, whether there is a spiritual realm at all and how acknowledging and incorporating such into one's life makes not only for a fuller human existence but for a more accurate view of reality, a more complete grasp of what's true. And yes, *if true*, that would certainly be so. But couldn't we bracket that belief as something that is there but has no real or significant impact on *most* of the goals we would seek and the actions we would take to make the world a better place to live?

No, we can't. That would just be ducking the question. Rather, we must ask *how* such a view of the spiritual might make a significant difference either in the <u>what</u> is to be sought or in <u>what means are best</u> in achieving the goal(s) sought.

As for *what* is to be sought, it comes down, mainly, to a view of what constitutes a fully-realized human being. And the RS would say: someone who knows (and strives to know) what's true and who tries to live their life in accordance with that truth. But the SH could certainly agree with that. The difference comes in what is thought to be true. For the RS, it's true that there is a spiritual realm and that that realm constitutes an important part of reality and of our own identity. They might, e.g., hold with Chardin as here:

> "We are not human beings having a spiritual experience;
> we are spiritual beings having a human experience."
> Pierre Teilhard de Chardin

Not so for the SH. But would that make any difference? It might. It might, e.g., create a space and a degree of respect for other people's efforts to comprehend and incorporate that reality into their lives. The SH could do the same of course but more as an instance of tolerance for people holding (what they consider to be) false beliefs. And does that difference make a difference? It would certainly seem to on a felt level. Respected vs. tolerated. (Fully admitting that the first has often <u>not</u> been lived by the various religious traditions.)

(2) And that brings us to intentions and motivations. Components critically involved in judging the character of any action. When determining the character, the quality, of any human action, we take more into account than just the physical components that go to make up the action. We also consider such things as the motivation(s) behind it, the intentions of the actor in undertaking it, even the beliefs of the actor which inform her choice of that particular action. All of these go into our assessment of the quality, the merit, the nobility,

due his or her behavior, from selfish to unselfish, ignoble to noble, hidden or apparent.

But giving both sides in our question here the benefit of any doubt, assume the intentions are equally unselfish and well-intentioned. Would there still be any difference in **the quality of the actions** taken? For the SH, presumably the motivation would be to make the world a better place because that would enable people to lead more fulfilling lives and to achieve greater happiness. It would lessen the overall amount of suffering in the world. The RS could agree with and accept such motivation but would probably also see such activity as obeying the will of God. But its not at all clear that such a difference would actually make any difference either in the actions chosen nor in how they were carried out. So, no difference then?

(3) No. I think there would still be a difference, a difference in the area of *hope*. For the RS, they firmly adopt a stance of hope. A hope that their activities in this effort will bear fruit. The SH might also hope for that but the difference is that for the RS, that hope is conjoined with *a trust* that it will indeed come to pass. Not so for the SH. But even if we grant this difference, does it make any difference in the actions chosen or to the recipients of those actions? Perhaps not. But it could easily make a difference to the actor, in such things as perseverance and positivity.

(4) And there is one final difference that seems to reflect the divergence in worldviews between the SH and the RS. And that has to do with the place of **suffering** in each. Both want to get rid of it or at least diminish it in their own lives and in the lives of others. But for the RS, it is somehow seen as also playing **a redemptive role**. It's not merely useless or simply a to-be-escaped-from characteristic of a physical

universe that runs according to fixed laws. Somehow, for the RS, it both reinforces their connection to other people (everybody undergoes suffering in one form or another) and elicits a response of wanting to relieve their suffering. In both of these ways, the existence of suffering **is redemptive** for the RS. It helps to redeem them from their self-centeredness and their selfishness. But with respect to these last two points– as to how suffering might be redemptive– couldn't it be equally so for the SH?

4) But doesn't that hope and trust we spoke of earlier necessarily lead to, require that, ultimately and finally good will prevail and suffering will have played a role in achieving that good?

Is there, then, and in the final analysis, any difference between the SH and the RS in how each strives to make the world a better place to live? The answer proposed here is: there may well be no *observable* difference between them either in the ends striven for or in the best means to achieve those ends. But there is likely a difference between them in the motivations and intentions that inform their actions, and that difference has to do with the context of hope and trust from which the RS's actions emanate.

And does that difference make any difference? Does it make any difference in **the ends striven for**? Aside from the obvious, i.e. any ends which involve a spiritual reality, no. And what about **the means used** to attain those ends? From a purely functional standpoint, no. But from the standpoint which includes motivations and intentions, very likely yes. And finally, there seems to be a significant difference between them in how they see and interpret suffering.

****

ACKNOWLEDGMENTS

There are many people to thank for their help in the creation and writing of this book. Some who are now alive and some who are long dead. I'll focus only on the "now alive" group.

First and foremost would be my wife, Karin E. Ringheim who took the time to carefully read each chapter and make both editorial-like comments and more substantive ones. Invariably, her comments were both helpful and thought-provoking. I am definitely in her debt on both accounts.

In addition to Karin, a small group was formed to read and comment on each chapter as it neared its final form. Their focus was primarily an editorial one. How could I make the chapter at hand read more easily and its contents and arguments be more easily followed and understood? What changes would they recommend to help accomplish both goals? And, again, I thought their recommendations did indeed enhance both the readability and content of the book. The main participants in this group were John Cunningham, Laura Mai Gainor, Steve McClure, Glenn Slocum, and Jim Doran. My thanks and debt goes out to all of them.

Made in the USA
Middletown, DE
17 February 2024

49907268R00085